Learn How to Study and SOAR to Success

Kenneth A. Kiewra
University of Nebraska–Lincoln

PEARSON
Prentice
Hall

Upper Saddle River, New Jersey
Columbus, Ohio

Library of Congress Cataloging-in-Publication Data

Kiewra, Kenneth A.
   Learn how to study and SOAR to success / Kenneth A. Kiewra.
      p. cm.
   Includes bibliographical references and index.
   ISBN 0-13-113562-7
   1. Study skills. 2. Learning strategies. I. Title.

LB1049.K56 2005
371.3'028`1—dc22

                          2004019258

Vice President and Publisher: Jeffery W. Johnston
Senior Acquisitions Editor: Sande Johnson
Editorial Assistant: Erin Anderson
Production Editor: Holcomb Hathaway
Design Coordinator: Diane C. Lorenzo
Cover Designer: Ali Mohrman
Cover Photo: SuperStock
Text Designer: Aerocraft Charter Art Service
Production Manager: Susan Hannahs
Director of Marketing: Ann Castel Davis
Marketing Manager: Amy Judd
Compositor: Carlisle Communications, Ltd.

Pearson Education Ltd.
Pearson Education Australia Pty. Limited
Pearson Education Singapore Pte. Ltd.
Pearson Education North Asia Ltd.

Pearson Education Canada, Ltd.
Pearson Education de Mexico, S. A. de C.V.
Pearson Education—Japan.
Pearson Education Malaysia Pte. Ltd.

ISBN 0-13-113562-7

DEDICATION

To Keaton, Anna, and Samuel: You've opened a world for me as pure, as beautiful, and as magical as Narnia. I've delighted in our adventures and cherished all you've given me along the way.

Brief Contents

Contents

Preface

You've heard it repeatedly throughout your academic life: "Study for the test." Sure, that directive has taken many forms. Perhaps your biology teacher said, "Big quiz Tuesday. Be sure you study." Maybe your history teacher said, "Know your names and dates for the midterm." Or, your psychology instructor might have said, "Review your lecture notes for the test on cognitive development." Whatever is said, you've been instructed or advised repeatedly to study for tests.

But, who's taught you how to study? Who's taught you how to record a good set of notes and how to review them? Probably no one. Schools teach content such as math and science but rarely teach students how to study that content. Isn't it odd that you've been in school this long, been expected to study since elementary school, but never been taught how to study?

So, how have you studied all this time? If you're like most students, you've studied using one or more of the RE-dundant study strategies such as RE-reading, RE-copying, RE-citing . . . , RE-diculous! You'll learn here that redundant strategies don't work very well. But you probably know this already. You've melodically recited the "Star Spangled Banner" with others hundreds of times. Try reciting it now, out loud, on your own. You've perhaps reread certain prayers hundreds of times. Try recalling them now from memory. You've certainly reviewed a dollar bill thousands of times. Try describing that bill now. Not so easy, huh? Redundant strategies are RE-diculous.

How should you study, then? This book, *Learn How to Study and SOAR to Success,* answers that question. It teaches you how to prepare an effective set of study notes and what to do with them. The SOAR acronym makes it easy to remember the steps:

S **S**elect Information

O **O**rganize Information

A **A**ssociate Information

R **R**egulate Learning

The SOAR steps are also easy to follow. Selecting information means recording a complete set of notes. Organizing information means constructing representations that reveal at a glance relationships among ideas. Associating information means drawing relationships among the ideas being learned, and relating ideas being learned to ideas already in memory. And, regulating learning means generating and answering practice test questions like those expected on the test.

Well, what makes SOAR so good or makes this study skills book better than other books? First, it provides a complete system for how to study—from note taking through test preparation. Other books provide you with an endless array of chapters and topics that never reveal a clear study process. This text teaches you *how* to study.

Second, this book is based on sound psychological theory and research. Many other books are not. Those familiar with educational psychology will recognize ideas such as constructivism, metacognition, structural knowledge, attribution theory, information processing, and self-regulated learning, even though those very terms might not appear in this book. You'll notice the application of research on note taking, knowledge representation, organization, elaboration, mnemonics, self-testing, and intrinsic and extrinsic motivation.

Moreover, I often pull from my own experiences as a researcher who has investigated note taking, studying, and knowledge representations for 20 years, and from my experiences directing an academic support center and teaching study skills classes. Many other study skills books are written by folks who teach classes in this area but who lack a scientific foundation.

But don't get the idea that you'll be bombarded here with theory and overwhelmed with research citations. Neither is visible. Theory and research are seamlessly woven throughout the book's ideas. A brief list of supplemental readings appears at the end of the book for those who wish to probe further.

Third, *SOAR* focuses on knowledge representations. My colleague Nelson DuBois and I developed and researched a simple system for representing information. Our representation system, covered in Chapter 3, helps you organize information and learn relationships within that information. Without such a system, students typically learn information in a disjointed, piecemeal fashion—one idea at a time—never noting how the ideas relate. The representation system is the cornerstone of the SOAR study system. Once you organize notes into representations, you then use those representations to create associations and to generate and answer practice test questions. One reviewer wrote: "Chapter 3 is the heart of the book. This chapter alone is worth the price of admission."

Fourth, the text adds or integrates other central topics. You might have thought that because the text focuses on the SOAR study system, other fundamental topics would be left uncovered. Not true. You'll find a chapter on motivation because successful students need both skill (like SOAR) and will. Time management has not been forgotten. Those principles are embedded in Chapter 7 because motivated students spend time striving for their goals. Time management ideas are also embedded in Chapter 6, which covers means for arranging a successful study routine. What about attention and test anxiety? They're embedded in Chapter 6 as well. Where's metacognition? That's largely the R (regulation) portion of SOAR addressed in Chapter 5. Error analysis is covered in that chapter, too. Reading, writing, and solving real-world problems are aided by SOAR strategies as well. Those topics are the focus of Chapter 8. And, what about the flawed beliefs students sometimes hold about learning? Those are challenged and dispelled throughout the book. You might be wondering where topics such as learning styles, left brain–right brain, speed reading, and sleep learning are found. Not here. Although these topics have garnered popular interest, there is insufficient scientific evidence supporting them. Just because an idea is popular does not necessarily make it useful.

Fifth, this book includes several design features that help you learn. Each chapter contains focus questions, headings, a summary, answers to focus questions, and practice exercises. Before you read a chapter, examine all of these. You're not actually expected to answer the focus questions before you read, however. They begin each chapter to help you focus your attention while you read. Complete the questions and exercises as or after you read the chapter to check your understanding and promote your skill development. Another helpful feature is the many exhibits appearing throughout the text. These demonstrate how to use the strategies you are learning. Don't skip over them. Pay close attention to them when they are mentioned in the text. Each chapter also includes an uproariously funny (okay, cute) opening scenario that often describes students like . . . friends of yours. These scenarios set the stage for what you'll learn in the chapter.

Finally, the book is written in what I hope is a clear, simple, straightforward, and entertaining way. I've made some occasional stabs at humor to make the book more fun. You'll no doubt see that these stabs barely scratch humor's surface.

A SPECIAL NOTE TO STUDENTS

There's one more really important thing I want to say to students about to read this book: When you're done reading it, don't resell it to the bookstore or a friend. I won't make a dime. Oops, that wasn't it. The really important thing is this: Be an assertive learner.

Let me tell you a little story. During my junior year of college I decided to take a three-week ornithology class because I had always been fascinated by the fluttering plumes of the bluebird of paradise, the whirling dance of the woodcock, and the twittering calls of the white-throated sparrow. Well, that's what I told my parents. I signed up for the class because Gloria Petuci did.

The class met Saturday mornings in the foothills surrounding Oneonta, New York. We stuffed knapsacks with binoculars, cameras, bird books, notebooks, canteens, and Freihoffer chocolate chip cookies. We traipsed through soggy fields and through narrow paths lined with poison sumac while looking for birds. We spotted and studied dozens of birds and endlessly noted boring facts about their habitats, appearance, songs, food-gathering methods, mating rituals, migration patterns, and many more things.

The three weeks flew by like a chicken and it was eventually test time. Our entire course grade was determined by this single test. The test was not at all what I or my classmates expected. The test contained only bird footprints—25 in all. Yes, just bird feet. We had to determine which bird made which print.

I guessed my way to a 68. The class average was 63. Everyone was outraged. Several students approached me and asked if I would talk to the professor on behalf of the class because of my background in educational psychology. I agreed to do it because I fundamentally believed that unfair test practices were rotting the very core of American education. That and because Gloria was one of the students who asked me to do it.

I tapped on the professor's door. He sat perched on a stiff wooden chair behind a large metal desk. "Come in," he squawked. "What do you want?"

"I was in your ornithology class and really liked it," I lied. "I want to talk with you about the test."

His eyes narrowed like a hawk's before it pounces on its prey. "Yes, what is it?"

"Uh well . . . the test seemed unfair," I stammered. "You taught us many wonderful things about birds but only tested us about their feet."

"That's quite enough, young man," the professor answered. "I don't want to hear any more criticism of my test."

I was speechless—like a canary staring at a cat. I almost flew the coop but then remembered why I came and what I stood for. "I've got to see this through," I thought. "It will really impress Gloria." I found the courage and the words. "Well, I'm in educational psychology and we learned about how tests must be valid—they have to test what was taught. And your test just wasn't."

"Young man, not another word or I'm reporting you to the dean," the professor crowed with arms flapping.

But there was no stopping me now. "It just wasn't a valid test," I wailed.

"That's it," he shrieked. "I'm reporting you to the dean. Tell me your name."

I calmly removed my shoes and socks, put my feet up on his desk, and said, "You tell me."

Okay, maybe it didn't happen exactly that way, and maybe that's a tad too assertive. But you get the idea: Students need to be responsible for themselves as learners.

Another quick story. I was teaching elementary school students how to play chess and was showing the moves of a game on a large demonstration board hanging on the wall. I eventually realized that some students off to one side could not see the board because of where I stood. I turned to them and asked, "Can you see?" "No," they said, "You're in the way." They could not see the game I was showing and yet they did nothing to solve their problem. I told them that they should move where they could see or should politely ask me to move, but that they should not sit there like clams on a beach. And neither should you. Be assertive. Take charge of your learning.

When the lecturer is speaking at about 860 words per minute and sparks shoot from your pencil as you scribble notes and try to keep pace, take charge. Politely ask the instructor to slow down or ask the instructor a question about the content. Instructors won't be angry; they'll be pleased that you're interested and trying hard to learn. Of course, there are things you can do to capture speedy information. You can tape-record the lecture and take notes at your own pace when you replay it and pause it later. You can meet with a study group later and compare and complete notes.

Or perhaps you feel frustrated preparing for a test because you have no idea what to expect. Take charge. Ask the instructor for a study guide or for advice on how to best prepare. Check with former students and confer with students in your class. Use the SOAR strategies presented in this text to help prepare for exams and anticipate test questions.

But, never, never sit idly by and simply let school happen to you. Be an assertive learner. It's up to you to make sure you learn.

Now, do all you can to learn and SOAR to success.

Acknowledgments

My sincere thanks to the many people whose influence helped shape *Learn How to Study and SOAR to Success*.

There was no greater influence than Dr. Nelson DuBois (State University of New York, Oneonta), my long-time mentor, collaborator, and friend. It was when I was a student in his undergraduate educational psychology class that I knew I wanted to become an educational psychologist like Dr. DuBois. His ideas are visible throughout the text, particularly those associated with representations and the DIFS motivation model.

I'm also indebted to four other long-time colleagues for all they taught me. Thank you Dr. Harold Fletcher (Florida State University), Dr. Stephen Benton (Kansas State University), Dr. Richard Mayer (University of California, Santa Barbara), and Dr. Joel Levin (University of Arizona).

Many current or former students contributed to the study of studying and helped shape my ideas. They include: Maribeth Christensen, Dave Christian, Patti Gubbels, Brent Igo, Doug Kauffman, Sung-II Kim, Jeff Lang, Matt McCrudden, Nancy Risch, Daniel Robinson, Rayne Sperling, and Scott Titsworth. I cherish the times we worked together and appreciate all you taught me.

This work was also strengthened by the thorough and thoughtful guidance of reviewers. Many thanks to the following reviewers for their helpful comments: Maribeth Long, Lock Haven University; Barbara Hofer, Middlebury College; Carey Harbin, Chabot College; Linda Blair, Pellissippi State Technical Community College; Carol Apt, South Carolina State University; Richard Mayer, University of California, Santa Barbara; Myron Dembo, University of Southern California; and Susan Knepley, Red Rocks Community College.

This book could not have been produced were it not for the many people who shared in its production. I thank Ken Jensen and Orville Friesen and the Instructional Design Center staff at the University of Nebraska for developing many of the graphics. A special thank you goes to Susan McCoy (also at Nebraska) for transforming the stack of handwritten pages into a professionally typed manuscript.

I also thank the outstanding Prentice Hall production staff who helped the ideas come to life. Special thanks to Senior Editor Sande Johnson and Editorial

Assistant Erin Anderson, who added this title to the Prentice Hall collection, offered bright ideas, and encouragingly led me through the publication process.

Most of all I recognize my family for guiding, supporting, and encouraging me at all times. My deepest appreciation goes to my parents, Frank and Winnifred; my siblings, Dard and Diane; my wife, Christine; and my children, Keaton, Anna, and Samuel.

About the Author

Kenneth A. Kiewra is a professor of educational psychology at the University of Nebraska–Lincoln. A graduate of Florida State University, Kiewra was also on the faculty at Kansas State University and Utah State University. Dr. Kiewra teaches courses and conducts research on learning and instruction. He is the editor of *Educational Psychology Review*. For fun, Dr. Kiewra enjoys running, coaching chess and soccer, and restoring antique minivans.

Lift Off to SOAR

1

Overview

Focus Questions

1. What percentage of important lecture ideas do students typically record in notes?

2. What strategy do students commonly use to review lecture notes?

3. Why don't students know how to learn?

4. What are two reasons why most teachers don't teach study strategies?

5. What should be done instead of rehearsal to study information?

6. What does SOAR stand for?

7. What does it mean to create internal associations? External associations?

8. How does one best regulate learning?

9. Identify each of the following questions as single fact, relational fact, or concept: (A) How are internal associations and external associations the same and different? (B). Marcy is learning about supply and demand. She relates this information to her own dismal experience selling ice cream at a football game during a snowstorm. What kind of association has Marcy made? (C) What does the S in SOAR stand for?

The coffeepot is working overtime. As Roger sips the night's fifth cup, the clock reads 3:35 A.M. Later this morning, at 10:00, Roger will take his second biology exam. Roger began studying at 7:30 P.M.—nearly a full eight hours ago—in hopes of posting a good grade. He needs one. Roger notched only a 62 percent on the first exam. But last time, Roger only studied until three in the morning. This time he's pulling an all-nighter.

Roger began this night's study by reading chapters 4 through 8 in the residence hall study lounge. He prefers to save reading assignments until the night before, so that the material is fresh in his mind. Roger was distracted a few times, though, by friends who just wanted to talk and by folks circulating through the lounge checking to see who was there.

Later, Roger met with six classmates to study. But by the time they'd finished griping about the instructor's boring lectures and lousy tests, the group members scarcely had time to exchange and copy each other's notes for missed lectures. Roger copied notes for five missed lectures and for a few when he had dozed off to sleep. One classmate needed notes from 14 lectures. She carted notebooks to a copy machine and dropped in about $20 in change to make copies. The group thought this was a hoot.

Now Roger is in his room, lying on the bed, rereading lecture notes that are nothing more than a few scattered terms with some half-baked definitions, for about the sixth time. He mindlessly recites the partial definitions of new terms such as *mitosis, meiosis, genotype,* and *phenotype* until he nods off to sleep. Roger dozes until the last drops of coffee sizzle in the pot, waking him from a DNA nightmare. The sun now lights the clock, which reads 9:25 A.M. Roger wipes the sleep from his eyes and concludes he's not cut out for all-nighters. He takes a quick shower, grabs a doughnut and cup of coffee, and heads to the exam.

Again, the exam is not what Roger expects. He doesn't have to define terms such as *mitosis* and *meiosis,* but he does have to identify new examples from illustrations. He doesn't have to define *genotype* or *phenotype,* but he does need to use these ideas to predict an offspring's characteristics. "Where does the instructor come up with these questions?" Roger wonders. Midway through the exam, Roger realizes he's toast and that even a C on this exam is a long shot. Roger yawns, pencils in another guess, and hopes he can hang on to his D average.

Janet, meanwhile, one of Roger's classmates, nailed the biology test: 97 percent. She was more familiar with mitosis and meiosis than her roommate's sweaters. She predicted an offspring's characteristics as effortlessly as predicting rubbery eggs in the dining hall's breakfast buffet.

Unlike Roger, Janet relaxed the night before the test. She shot hoops in the rec center, listened to some Backstreet Boys, and turned in early. Why not? Janet was ready for the test days ago. She studied throughout the semester alone in her room and with her study group in the library. This group was as serious as the royal guards at the Tower of London. And, Janet used effective study strategies. She took complete notes, organized them, made associations, and regulated her learning by testing herself in advance of the test.

Janet was not always a successful and serious student, though During Janet's freshman year her grade point average (GPA) was barely divisible by one. Her scholastic future was as bleak as a bank robber with vanity plates. Janet hated studying more than her roommate's boyfriend. After a while, Janet gave up studying and played her favorite game, Playstation 2—NCAA Football, almost constantly.

Eventually, eye to eye with academic probation, Janet saw her way into an academic skills class that taught students how to study. For Janet and others in the class, the study strategies taught were surprisingly new. Janet wondered why she had not been taught how to study earlier. Had teachers covered all this back in sixth grade the day Janet ditched school and went fishing, leaving her to flounder ever since? Janet finally learned, for the first time, to record complete notes, organize them using charts and illustrations, associate ideas with each other and to things she already knew, and to test herself prior to the exam.

Janet first put the study strategies to the test in her chemistry class in the weeks preceding the first exam. When she eventually strode into the test room, Janet was as certain that she could make an A as she could pass for over 300 yards against any team in the Mid-American Conference.

During the next class, the chemistry teacher looked sour when he announced that the test scores ranged from 37 to 94, and that the class average was an abysmal 67. He inquired where the party had been.

But Janet had scored a 94! When she learned that, she wasn't really surprised. She knew she had mastered the material by using effective study strategies.

After that, Janet's passing yardage leveled off but her GPA came up quicker than a diver with a broken air hose. Her 94 in chemistry was followed by an unbroken string of high grades throughout her educational career including that 97 percent on the biology test. Janet enjoyed her high grades and her newfound interest in learning. Moreover, she was relieved at being set free from the frustration of trying to study when she really didn't know how.

INEFFECTIVE STUDY TECHNIQUES

Does Roger remind you of anyone? Maybe yourself? Roger reminds me of many students I've worked with as director of the Academic Success Center at the University of Nebraska and as instructor for the class "Strategies for Academic Success." I've found that most students study ineffectively for tests. Like Roger, they study

- at the wrong time—just prior to the test
- in the wrong place—in noisy and distracting places such as study lounges
- with the wrong people—other poorly prepared students
- for the wrong reasons—solely to pass the test
- using ineffective materials—incomplete and unorganized notes
- using ineffective strategies—sketchy note taking and rehearsing definitions

In short, when most students are asked "when, where, with whom, why, what, and how should you study?" They don't have a clue. This text answers all these studying questions—particularly the "how" question.

Let's glimpse for a moment at just how most students study. First off, studying actually begins when students first acquire the material they'll later review for the test. Oftentimes, that material is acquired by selecting key ideas and recording them in lecture notes during classroom lectures. We'll begin, then, by looking at a brief lecture on animal behavior and a student's resulting lecture notes.

Animal Behavior

The study of animal behavior is approached in contrasting ways by two types of psychologists: comparative psychologists and ethologists.

Comparative psychologists can be compared with ethologists along several dimensions. Comparative psychologists study animal behavior in laboratory settings. They conduct diligent experiments on a few animal species, trying to uncover general learning principles common to all animals. These American psychologists believe that behavior is learned.

Ethologists, on the other hand, study animal behavior in the animal's natural surroundings. Their methods are less rigorous. They usually observe animals. Ethologists study many animals to learn how each behaves. These European psychologists believe that behavior is innate.

Now, let's look at a typical set of notes students might record during that brief lecture on animal behavior.

Animal Behavior
Comparative Psychologists
    – Study animals
    – Conduct experiments
    – American
Ethologists
    – Natural surroundings
    – Observe
    – Innate

Look familiar? Imagine studying these sketchy notes weeks later while reviewing for a test. There is a lot of incomplete or missing information that can never be reviewed because it was never noted. For instance:

Comparative Psychologists . . .

- study animals in laboratories
- study only a few animals
- try to uncover general laws common to all animals
- believe behavior is learned
- are American psychologists

Ethologists . . .

- study animal behavior
- study animals in their natural surroundings
- use methods that are less rigorous
- study many animals to learn how each behaves
- believe behavior is innate
- are European psychologists

That's a lot of information to omit from notes, but it's not surprising. Students typically record in notes only about 40 percent of important lecture ideas.

Exercise 1

Take out your class notebooks and examine your notes. Are they complete and understandable? Using your notes could you reconstruct the entire lecture? How could these notes be improved?

As if having sketchy notes to review isn't bad enough, students typically review them in a weak and ineffective manner—rehearsal. They recite the few facts they have recorded over and over. Rehearsal, contrary to popular belief, does not produce long-term learning. Rehearsed facts are commonly forgotten ("I've forgotten where comparative psychologists work"), confused with related facts ("Ethologists conduct experiments"), or difficult to apply in new settings ("I have no idea what type of psychologist a bird-watcher might be").

Recording sketchy notes and rehearsing them—the prevailing student study methods—leave you as lost as most $20 pens come test time. As you'll soon learn, there are far more effective ways to study. But, first, let's address why students like Roger and you, who have attended school for many years and taken hundreds of tests, still might not know how to study.

WHY STUDENTS USE INEFFECTIVE STUDY TECHNIQUES

Instruction and practice are needed to learn golf and learn study strategies.

The main reason you might not know how to study effectively is that no one taught you how. Think back over your school years. Remember all the times your teachers announced, "You have a math test on Tuesday," or suggested, "Study for your history test on Friday," but never told you how to study? Strange, isn't it? It's because schools teach students content such as math and history but rarely teach them how to learn such content. Has anyone, for instance, taught you how to select and note important ideas, how to organize them, how to associate them with each other and with things you already know, and how to construct and answer practice test items to regulate learning? Probably not. Most schools do not offer classes on how to study, and teachers rarely teach study strategies while teaching their subject matter.

So, why don't teachers teach study strategies? Perhaps there are two reasons. First, most teachers, as students, were never taught how to study either. Thus, many teachers are not qualified to teach study strategies. Second, many teachers falsely believe that strategy instruction is remedial—something for correcting faulty study habits. But, how can instruction in how to study be remedial if study strategy instruction never occurred in the first place? Of course, it can't, but still many educators believe strategy instruction is remedial because they assume that most students acquire study strategies as naturally as they acquire height and weight. That's wrong. They don't. You learn study strategies the same way Tiger Woods learned a fluid golf swing: through instruction and practice. Without instruction in how to study, most students pick up weak, sloppy strategies such as sketchy note taking and rehearsal, just as an untrained golfer develops an awkward swing.

I should know. I began playing golf when I was 10, and although I played and practiced several times a year, I never improved very much. Finally, when I was in college, I took a series of lessons from a golf pro. It was amazing how much I learned and how quickly I improved after that. Subtle little pointers she provided such as "Remove the head cover from the driver before teeing off" and "Hold the club by the handle on the other end" helped me cut several strokes from my handicap. You see my point. Practice alone—in golf or studying—won't do it. Instruction is needed to put you on course.

In summary, you probably need instruction in how to study because you weren't born with these skills and probably nobody, to date, has taught you how to study. Thus, reading this book and learning how to study is hardly a remedial task. Rather, it is an enriching task because once you are finally taught how to study, like Janet, you'll be able to learn anything anytime.

Exercise 2

Think about your own school career. Write down everything you can remember being taught in school about note taking, organizing notes, and studying for tests.

EFFECTIVE STUDY TECHNIQUES

Let me offer a quick sample of what is possible when you know how to study using the animal behavior material presented earlier. First, you'll *select* all the important lecture ideas and record them in notes. You'll have a complete set of notes like those shown in Exhibit 1.1.

Second, you'll *organize* the important information as shown in Exhibit 1.2. Wouldn't it be great to have notes like this to study?

EXHIBIT 1.1   Notes for animal behavior lecture.

Animal Behavior

Comparative Psychologists
- Study animal behavior
- Conduct studies in laboratories
- Conduct experiments on few animals
- Try to uncover general learning principles
- Are American psychologists
- Believe behavior is learned

(continued)

EXHIBIT 1.1   Notes for animal behavior lecture. (continued)

Ethologists
- Study animal behavior
- Study in animals' natural surroundings
- Use observation methods
- Study many animals
- Try to learn how each animal behaves
- Are European psychologists
- Believe behavior is innate

EXHIBIT 1.2   Organized notes for animal behavior lecture.

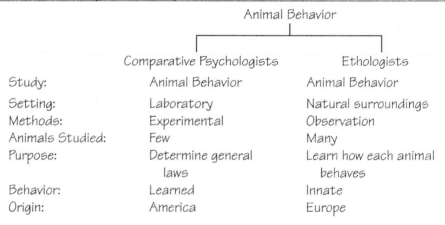

	Comparative Psychologists	Ethologists
Study:	Animal Behavior	Animal Behavior
Setting:	Laboratory	Natural surroundings
Methods:	Experimental	Observation
Animals Studied:	Few	Many
Purpose:	Determine general laws	Learn how each animal behaves
Behavior:	Learned	Innate
Origin:	America	Europe

Third, you won't meaninglessly rehearse isolated facts over and over, trying to pound them into your brain. Instead, you'll *associate* the new ideas with each other and with things you already know. Following are some sample associations:

- Experimental methods and laboratories go together because experiments usually take place in laboratories.
- The observation method is associated with natural surroundings; you would want to unobtrusively observe what animals do in their natural setting.
- Comparative psychologists study few (animals) to understand many; ethologists study many to understand few (each).
- Famous comparative psychologists include Thorndike and Skinner. Darwin was an ethologist.
- I'll remember that ethologists work in Europe because both begin with the letter *E*.
- Comparative psychologists use hard science (experiments in laboratories), whereas ethologists use soft science (observation in natural settings).

- Watching how wolves forage is an example of ethology.
- Testing how quickly rats can run a maze with or without reinforcement is an example of comparative psychology.
- It seems that comparative psychologists favor nurture and ethologists favor nature in the nature–nurture debate.

Finally, you won't wait for the test to find out if you know the material. You'll *regulate* your own learning by generating and answering practice test questions in advance of the test. You'll know whether you know the information before the teacher tests you. Below are some practice items you might develop.

Answer C (for Comparative psychologist), E (for Ethologist), or B (for Both) for each item below:

___ 1. Born in America.
___ 2. Believes behavior is innate.
___ 3. Studies animal behavior.
___ 4. Works mostly in laboratory setting.
___ 5. Studies a few animals.
___ 6. Derives general laws.
___ 7. Watches bees pollinate to learn about bee pollination.
___ 8. Tests to see if pigeons can be made aggressive when punished.

Selecting all the important information, **O**rganizing it, **A**ssociating it, and **R**egulating learning by self-testing are highly effective strategies well within your reach. Collectively, they comprise the SOAR study system detailed throughout this book.

THE SOAR STUDY SYSTEM

You've seen that recording sketchy notes and rehearsing them is no way to study for tests. Like Janet, you need to SOAR to success. The remainder of this chapter introduces you more formally to the four SOAR components: Select, Organize, Associate, and Regulate. You see the SOAR system at work for studying new lecture material on reinforcement schedules. Chapters 2 through 5 each address one component of the SOAR system in more detail. Let's lift off to SOAR.

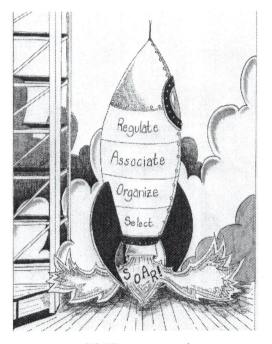

SOAR to success!

Select Information

The first step in studying is to select all the important information and record a complete set of notes to review. Complete means that notes contain all key terms, definitions, examples, and details. Most students never have complete lecture notes to review because they record only about 40 percent of the important information. That's ineffective because information not contained in notes has only about a 5 percent chance of being recalled on a test.

Following is a brief lecture on schedules of reinforcement, another important topic in psychology. Following that, in Exhibit 1.3, you'll see two sets of notes— incomplete notes presented on the left side and complete notes presented on the right side. Note that the complete set contains all the key terms, definitions, examples, and details that the student selected and noted. Which set of notes would you rather have when reviewing for a test?

Schedules of Reinforcement

Okay, class, we've just covered reinforcement. Now, we'll see that there are different schedules one might use in delivering reinforcement.

Suppose you have a pigeon and you want to train it to peck a key. To train the pigeon, you give it food pellets for pecking the correct keys. There are four main schedules you can use to deliver the reinforcement. The type of schedule used determines several things about the animal's behavior.

Fixed-interval schedules deliver reinforcement following the first response after a fixed time interval. The pigeon, for example, might receive food for its first peck after a 10-second interval. Fixed-interval schedules produce slow response rates that contain pauses in responding. The animal tends to pause after it's reinforced and then increase responding as the interval ends, because reinforcement is again anticipated. It is relatively easy to extinguish (eliminate) behaviors learned on this schedule.

Variable-interval schedules deliver reinforcement following the first response after a predetermined but variable time interval. The pigeon, for example, might receive food following intervals of 5, 15, 2, and 18 seconds for an average interval of 10 seconds. Variable-interval schedules produce slow but steady response rates. It is difficult to extinguish behaviors learned on this schedule.

Fixed-ratio schedules deliver reinforcement following a fixed number of responses. The pigeon, for example, might receive food following every 10 key pecks. Fixed-ratio schedules produce rapid responding, although the animal pauses briefly following reinforcement. It is relatively easy to extinguish behaviors learned on this schedule.

Variable-ratio schedules deliver reinforcement after a predetermined but variable number of responses. The pigeon, for example, might receive food after making 5, 15, 2, and 18 pecks for an average ratio of 10 pecks. Variable-ratio schedules produce rapid and steady responding. It is difficult to extinguish behaviors learned on this schedule.

EXHIBIT 1.3   *Incomplete compared with complete notes.*

Incomplete Notes	Complete Notes
Schedules of Reinforcement	Schedules of Reinforcement

Fixed Interval
   Reinforcement after first
   response
   Slow pauses
   Extinguish
	Fixed Interval
	   Definition—reinforce first
	   response after a fixed time
	   interval
	   Example—food for first key peck
	   after 10 s
	   Response rate—slow, pauses
	   Extinction—relatively easy

Variable Interval
   First response
   Slow, steady
   Difficult
	Variable Interval
	   Definition—reinforce first re-
	   sponse after predetermined but
	   variable interval
	   Example—food for first key peck
	   after 5, 15, 2, and 18 s
	   Response rate—slow, steady
	   Extinction—difficult

Fixed Ratio
   Fixed number
   Rapid
   Extinguish
	Fixed Ratio
	   Definition—reinforce after fixed
	   number of responses
	   Example—food after every 10 key
	   pecks
	   Response Rate—rapid, pauses
	   Extinction—relatively easy

Variable Ratio
   Variable
   Rapid, steady
   Difficult
	Variable Ratio
	   Definition—reinforce after prede-
	   termined but variable number of
	   responses
	   Example—food after 5, 15, 2,
	   and 18 key pecks
	   Response rate—rapid, steady
	   Extinction—difficult

Having complete notes like those in Exhibit 1.3 to study is important because you can't study what you don't have. But a good set of study notes should also be well organized in order to help you make associations and learn relationships among noted ideas. Organizing notes is the next step in SOAR.

Organize Information

Notes can be better organized by creating representations like the matrix for schedules of reinforcement shown in Exhibit 1.4. Matrices are powerful organizational devices because they transform linear, listlike notes into powerful two-dimensional notes. Note that you can read the matrix in two directions: vertically by its four topics (fixed interval, variable interval, fixed ratio, and variable ratio) and horizontally by its categories (definition, example, response rate, and extinction). This two-dimensional format makes it easy to compare the topics along their various categories and create associations that are difficult to see in the linear notes students typically study. Take a good look at the matrix. Wouldn't you want to study it for a test?

EXHIBIT 1.4   *Matrix representation allowing easy comparisons across topics.*

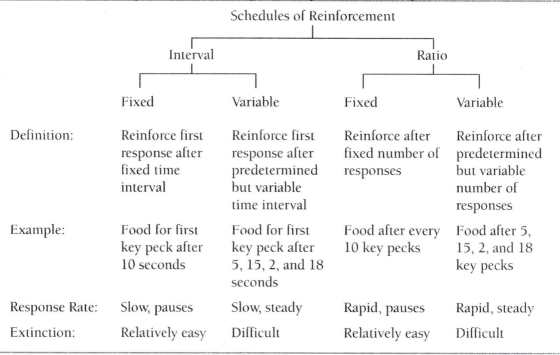

	Interval		Ratio	
	Fixed	Variable	Fixed	Variable
Definition:	Reinforce first response after fixed time interval	Reinforce first response after predetermined but variable time interval	Reinforce after fixed number of responses	Reinforce after predetermined but variable number of responses
Example:	Food for first key peck after 10 seconds	Food for first key peck after 5, 15, 2, and 18 seconds	Food after every 10 key pecks	Food after 5, 15, 2, and 18 key pecks
Response Rate:	Slow, pauses	Slow, steady	Rapid, pauses	Rapid, steady
Extinction:	Relatively easy	Difficult	Relatively easy	Difficult

Exercise 3

Below is a set of notes. Try to organize them better.

Prejudice and Discrimination

Discrimination—an action, unfair treatment toward someone
Prejudice—an attitude, a prejudging
    Positive prejudice—exaggerates the virtues of a group
    Negative prejudice—prejudgment that groups are inferior
Discrimination usually the result of prejudice
Sometimes prejudice and discrimination match or don't match

1. All-weather bigot—prejudiced and discriminates. Person might say, "Of course I discriminate—they deserve it."
2. Fair-weather bigot—prejudiced but does not discriminate. "I don't like them, but I can't turn them away."
3. Fair-weather liberal—not prejudiced but does discriminate—A server at a restaurant may be told to provide slower service to a group. Doing so, the server might remark, "What can I do? I don't want to get fired."
4. All-weather liberal—not prejudiced and does not discriminate. "Everyone should be treated equally. Anything less is un-American and immoral. I would never be part of it."

Associate Information

When you study, strive to associate information in two ways: create associations among the ideas being learned (internal associations) and create associations between the new ideas being learned and past knowledge (external associations). Remember that internal means *within* the ideas being learned, whereas external means *beyond* the ideas being learned.

Take a look at Exhibit 1.5. You see a student learning from a page of text. The broken lines joining the text ideas (the Xs) are internal associations. For example, a student reading about drugs for a health class makes the internal association that both Schedule I and Schedule II drugs are similar because both have high potential for abuse, but are different because Schedule I drugs have no medical use whereas Schedule II drugs have restricted medical use. The solid lines drawn from the text ideas to past information stored in the learner's memory (the triangles) are external associations. In this case, the student might associate Schedule I drugs with an already familiar drug such as heroin and associate Schedule II drugs with morphine.

EXHIBIT 1.5   *Internal and external associations.*

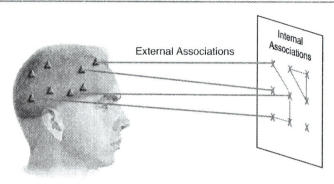

Create Internal Associations

Creating internal associations is like putting together a puzzle. At first, the pieces lie scattered and unconnected. The puzzler connects two pieces associated in color or shape. Eventually, several associated pieces are assembled to form the big picture that can be seen only when the pieces are properly arranged. Once completed, the puzzler no longer sees individual pieces but a meaningful scene—perhaps geese alighting on a frozen pond in a snowy meadow.

The matrix for schedules of reinforcement organizes or assembles the many pieces of information about schedules of reinforcement, making it easy to now create internal associations among the lecture pieces. Try it. Examine the reinforcement matrix and create internal associations among its many details. See if you can reveal the big picture.

Did you notice the following internal associations?

- Interval methods are based on time; ratio methods are based on number.
- In fixed methods, the reinforcement pattern remains constant; in variable methods, the reinforcement pattern changes.
- Interval methods produce slow responding; ratio methods produce rapid responding.
- Fixed methods produce pauses in responding; variable methods produce steady responding.
- Fixed methods are easy to extinguish; variable methods are difficult to extinguish.

Once you have made these internal associations, the material is easier to understand and remember than if you had simply examined and rehearsed each lecture detail in a piecemeal fashion. Now, the big picture is complete.

Exercise 4

Return to the organized notes you created on prejudice and discrimination. Now create internal associations.

Create External Associations

As a reminder, creating external associations means linking new information to ideas outside the material being learned—hence the name *external* associations. When creating external associations, you connect the ideas being learned to outside knowledge already in your memory. For example, when first learning about the principle of supply and demand you might relate it to knowledge you have about coins: the rarest ones, in least supply, are in highest demand and value. As was true with internal associations, creating external associations makes new information more understandable and memorable.

Let's see what external associations we can create for the material on schedules of reinforcement. We'll start by relating each schedule to a familiar example:

- *Fixed ratio.*   A salesperson who receives a commission for every five products sold is reinforced on a fixed-ratio schedule.
- *Variable ratio.*   Checking the coin return on a vending machine pays off on a variable-ratio schedule.
- *Fixed interval.*   Teachers who evaluate students using just midterm and final exams are using a fixed-interval schedule. As a result, students' studying behavior (response rate) is predictably "paused" for most of the semester except in the days just prior to testing.
- *Variable interval.*   Teachers who evaluate students using pop quizzes are using a variable-interval schedule. As a result, students' studying behavior is "steady" throughout the semester because they never know when a quiz is forthcoming.

Other external associations can be created to help remember this lecture information. Here is a sample:

- To remember that *fixed* schedules are *easy* to extinguish, remember that when you *fix* something in gambling it's *easy* to win.
- To remember that *variable* schedules are *difficult* to extinguish, remember that something *variable*, such as weather, is *difficult* to predict.
- To remember that *ratio* schedules produce *rapid responding,* remember the three *R*s: *ratio, rapid,* and *responding* (not reading, writing, and arithmetic).

When you create external associations, you hook new information (to be learned) with previous knowledge already stored in memory. This association makes the new information better understood and easier to retrieve from memory.

Exercise 5

Return again to your organized notes on prejudice and discrimination. Now create external associations.

Regulate Learning

Up to this point, you have studied by selecting and recording key ideas, organizing them, and creating internal and external associations. The final SOAR step is to regulate learning. You regulate learning by monitoring and controlling it. The best way to do this is by testing yourself. Generate and answer test questions like those you would expect on a test (more on predicting test questions in Chapter 5). Through this self-regulation process, there will be nothing your instructor can ask you that you have not already asked yourself. Oh, what a confident feeling that should bring.

For the test on schedules of reinforcement, we can predict three possible types of questions:

* *Single-fact questions.*   Requiring that you know a single fact.
* *Relational-fact questions.*   Requiring that you know relationships among facts.
* *Concept questions.*   Requiring that you recognize new examples.

Here are some sample questions you might generate and answer for each type of question:

Single-Fact Questions

* What is the definition for variable-interval schedules? (Reinforcement following a variable number of responses)
* Extinction is _____ to carry out for fixed-ratio schedules. (Easy)
* What is the response rate for variable-ratio schedules? (Slow and steady)

Relational-Fact Questions

* Which schedules involve steady responding? (Variable)
* Which schedules involve pauses following reinforcement? (Fixed)
* Which schedules are difficult to extinguish? (Variable)

Concept Questions

* In Fraü Heibert's German class, students listen to and repeat German conversation in a listening laboratory with personal headphones and

microphones. Fraü Heibert can listen in on any student at any time and reinforce him or her for responding appropriately. What type of reinforcement schedule is at work? (Variable interval)

- Bobby is solving chess problems using a computer program. Every time he solves five problems correctly the computer responds, "You're the champ, Bobby." What might you predict about how fast and steady Bobby's responses will be? (Rapid responding with pauses)

You should find that your practice questions are much like the actual test questions, because once you have selected and noted all the important content, organized it, and created associations among the ideas and with prior knowledge, it is easy to generate practice tests comparable with the real ones. And what better way to regulate learning than by constructing and answering testlike questions?

Exercise 6

Return once more to your notes and associations on prejudice and discrimination. Use these to generate single-fact, relational-fact, and concept questions for that material.

SUMMARY

Students have not been taught how to learn. Schools teach content such as math and science but not how to learn that content. Consequently, students use ineffective study strategies such as recording sketchy notes and later rehearsing those notes. They try to memorize facts in a piecemeal fashion. Instead, students should SOAR to success.

The SOAR study system makes sense and is easy to use. First, select the important content (S) by recording all the important information in notes. Second, organize the information (O) using representations whenever possible. Third, create associations (A) by linking noted ideas to each other (internal associations) and to prior knowledge (external associations). Finally, regulate learning (R) by generating and answering practice test questions.

In the following chapters, you'll learn more about how to SOAR. Chapter 2 covers selecting and noting information. Chapter 3 covers how to best organize noted information. Chapter 4 covers creating internal and external associations. And Chapter 5 covers regulating learning. Select, Organize, Associate, and Regulate and you'll SOAR to success.

ANSWERS TO FOCUS QUESTIONS

1. Students typically record only 40 percent of important lecture ideas.

2. Students commonly use rehearsal strategies to review lecture notes.

3. Students don't know how to learn because most teachers don't teach them how to learn. They teach content but not how to learn that content.

4. Most teachers don't teach study strategies because they've never been taught how to study either and because many teachers believe that strategy instruction is remedial.

5. Rather than rehearsal, students should build meaningful associations among the ideas being studied and associate those new ideas with things they already know. Also, students should regulate their learning by generating and answering practice test questions when studying.

6. SOAR stands for select information (S), organize information (O), associate information (A), and regulate learning (R).

7. Creating internal associations means finding relationships within the material being learned. Creating external associations means building relationships between material being learned and material previously learned.

8. One best regulates learning by developing and answering questions similar to those anticipated on a test. One tries to test oneself thoroughly in advance of the test.

9. A. Relational fact
   B. Concept
   C. Single fact

Select Information

2

Focus Questions

1. What are the two reasons that note taking is important?

2. Are most students good note takers?

3. What are the four things students should BE doing BEfore lectures?

4. How should students prepare physically, mentally, and emotionally for lectures?

5. Match the four GETS—GET it all, GET it fast, GET it now, and GET it again—to the following strategies. One has two answers.

  A. Use abbreviations and notations.

  B. Ask questions and for clarifications.

  C. Record main ideas, examples, and details.

  D. Replay recorded lectures.

  E. Pay attention to lecture cues.

6. How should students fill UP and fix UP after a lecture?

7. What are three problems associated with text highlighting?

Lanny glances nervously at his watch as he approaches the double doors of Lecture Hall 338. "Seven minutes past nine. I'm late for history class!" Still puffing from dashing across campus and running up three flights of stairs, Lanny fills his lungs with oxygen and his heart with courage and then slowly pulls open the door.

The door creaks and groans like a wood floor protesting under steps in the night. Instantly, 200 sets of eyes turn and flash at him, paralyzing him like a frightened deer frozen in a car's headlights. Another deep breath. Lanny shuffles down the aisle and across a crowded back row toward a vacant seat. He utters a litany of "Excuse me"s and "I'm sorry"s as he jostles three desks and stamps the feet of would-be note takers.

Lanny sifts through his bulging backpack, looking for his history notebook. "Chemistry . . . literature . . . algebra . . . why do they all look alike? . . . Ah! history!" Lanny flips to a page free from half-written letters and phone numbers. He rustles through his backpack once more, searching for a pen. A well-chewed ballpoint surfaces, but it has no ink in it. More rummaging. Finally, a pencil stub emerges. Predictably, it has a rounded point and no eraser.

At last, Lanny tunes in the instructor, who is droning on about Constantine the Great. "I've never heard this name before. How great could he be?" Lanny wonders. "Maybe the instructor introduced this character during the last lecture, when I overslept and missed class altogether . . . " Lanny muses.

The next several minutes are abuzz with names, dates, and places Lanny's never heard before. His brain drifts in and out and his notes, like the lines on an electroencephalogram, reflect his mental lapses. He records only occasional and meaningless notes—Armenia . . . Constantinople . . . Persians in 364 . . . Alaric—notes that capture the instructor's historical story the way a chain link fence captures water.

The instructor now flips on the overhead projector, showing a time line. Lanny strains to make out the distorted image, which seems light-years from where he's sitting at the rear of the lecture hall. He tilts his glasses nearer his eyes, hoping he can focus the image. He begins to copy what little he can see. Meanwhile, the instructor jabbers on about the significance of these events. Lanny copies, listens, copies, listens. Having only one brain, he does neither very well. Then, before he can fully observe it, the time line slide flickers and goes black, like a falling star in the night sky.

On and on the lecturer drones about the House of Theodosius, Sister Pulcheria, and husband Marcian. Lanny's attention shifts about the room to swinging legs, tapping pens, chesty coughs reminiscent of his bout with bronchitis, and the rustle of newspapers. The rustle reminds Lanny to renew his subscription to *USA Today*. He jots a reminder in his notebook.

Lanny's anguish and frustration with the lecture, though, are quickly buoyed by the sound of the closing bell. He inspects his notebook page, which contains about a half-page of notes—mostly names he cannot pronounce, spell, or explain—and proudly closes his notebook. As he leaves, Lanny notices several groups of students huddled together discussing and revising their lecture notes. "No time for that," Lanny thinks. "Literature begins in 15 minutes. That gives me almost enough time to renew my newspaper subscription and run across campus to the snack bar for a soda and bagel. Lectures sure are draining!"

Lanny's fictional lecture hall nightmare is, unfortunately, a reality for many students who fail to learn from lectures because, like Lanny, they fail to select important lecture ideas for further study. How can you possibly select key ideas when you miss or show up late for class, spend class time searching for materials, lack background knowledge about the topic, daydream, sit where it's difficult to see and hear, overtax your brain trying to listen and copy at the same time, become distracted by things happening around you, and record sketchy notes? You can't. Learning does not work that way. It works when you work. And, your learning work begins by selecting and holding on to the key ideas presented. If you don't, you have nothing to study later.

Note taking is the key to selecting information—for two reasons. First, note taking makes you more attentive. When you are busy taking notes, you don't have time to daydream or become bored. And, when you are focused on note taking, you are less likely to become distracted by other sights and sounds. Students who record lecture notes are more attentive and learn more than students who simply listen to the lecture without recording notes.

Second, note taking is important because it creates a permanent record of the ideas selected—a record that can be further studied even months later when preparing for a test. Many students shun note taking believing that they'll easily remember what they hear or read. Not so. Humans quickly forget much of what they experience even when they make a mental note to remember it. Mental notes fade quickly; written notes endure.

It is important, then, to record notes while learning. Note taking helps you focus attention on the information you should select, and it provides for further study a permanent record of what you've selected. The problem is that most students don't take full advantage of their note-taking opportunity. As stated in Chapter 1, most students select and record only about 40 percent of important lecture ideas and some students don't even record that many notes. This is unfortunate because the more ideas students note, the better they perform on tests. Furthermore, information not recorded in notes has only a 5 percent chance of being recalled later on a test. When it comes to recording lecture ideas, then, don't

Taking notes focuses your attention during the lecture.

be too selective. Strive to record a complete and detailed set of notes useful for further study.

This is probably the right time to tell the story of how I became interested in researching note taking. I was a graduate student at Florida State University enrolled in a statistics class. The professor, Dr. Fletcher, insisted that students *not* take notes during class for two reasons. First, he believed that note taking was distracting and interfered with listening, and, second, he provided students with a complete set of study notes following each lecture.

I was uncomfortable with his policy—having found note taking personally rewarding—so I became a closet note taker. I secretly took notes when Dr. Fletcher was not looking. Sometimes the urge to record notes even when he was looking was too great and I had to resort to trickery: "Dr. Fletcher, there's someone at the door looking for you," I fibbed. He'd look away and I'd write feverishly. One time he caught me pen handed! "Mr. Kiewra," he barked, "are you taking notes?" "No, sir," I sheepishly remarked, "I'm writing a letter to a friend back home." "Oh, okay," he relented. "I thought you were taking notes."

I went on to find that Dr. Fletcher was half wrong and half right about note taking. He was wrong about the process of note taking interfering with learning. As already mentioned, students who record lecture notes are more attentive and learn more than those not recording notes even when notes are not reviewed. He was right about the value of the notes he provided. Students perform well when they have a complete set of notes to study and, in most cases, notes provided by the instructor are far more complete than those students record.

Keep this story in mind to reinforce the idea that you should take complete notes. Taking notes focuses your attention during the lecture and provides you with a complete record of the lecture for further study. So, come out of the closet and take notes (and a lot of them) proudly.

The bulk of this chapter, then, tells you how to select and note lecture information. Doing so is crucial because lecture information is fleeting—you must select and record key ideas at that moment or they are gone forever. The last part of the chapter tells you how to select and note text information.

SELECTING AND NOTING LECTURE INFORMATION

There are things you can do before, during, and after a lecture to improve the selection and notation of information.

Before the Lecture

Believe it or not, there are things you can do before the lecture even starts to increase and improve note taking. Remember to do these four BEs—BE there, BE on time, BE up front, and BE on the edge—BEfore lectures.

1. BE There!

You must physically be there in class to learn from lectures. Course handouts, the textbook, and even fellow students' notes cannot completely recapture missed lecture information. Furthermore, your absence means you forfeit your opportunity to ask questions and contribute to class discussions. Classes should be experienced, not just attended. Are you as satisfied having a friend tell you about a movie or ballgame that you missed as you would be if you had experienced it yourself?

Sure, students have reasons for missing class, such as a dead car battery, a scheduled job interview, or illness. But are these reasons or excuses? If you discover that your car's battery is dead, run or ride a bike to class, or call a cab. Who scheduled the interview . . . the governor? No matter how important other commitments are or seem to be, schedule them outside class hours. If you're really sick, then stay home and do all that you can to recover quickly. Meanwhile, definitely arrange for a classmate to tape-record or videotape the lecture for you. But, if your illness is not contagious and you can sit up in bed, then you probably can sit up in class and should be there.

Also, don't get caught in the Absolution Delusion. The Absolution Delusion occurs when you ask your instructor if it's okay to miss a class for some reason—maybe an athletic event, a student council meeting, or a family trip—and the instructor says it's okay, thereby pardoning you from your lecture-skipping "sin." Although missing class may be permissible, it's still a dangerous practice because you're missing valuable information.

2. BE on Time!

Don't be late for classes. In fact, arrive extra early. Spend this time before class begins preparing your note-taking materials and reviewing previous notes. Furthermore, slipping into class late is inconsiderate to fellow students and the instructor, all of whom are hard at work.

There's really no excuse for being late. "I'm not a morning person" is certainly no excuse for showing up late to a 7:30 A.M. class. How would that excuse play in the army when presented to your drill sergeant? If 7:30 seems too early, then rise well beforehand, exercise, and eat a healthy breakfast. I guarantee you won't feel tired at 7:30. The old "couldn't find a parking place" is a feeble excuse too. Arrive plenty early, when parking spaces are readily available. Explore other means of transportation such as walking, biking, and carpooling. For every problem, there is a solution!

As is true with absences, if you're late, you miss out on what's happening in class and you cannot record notes. Thus, you miss out on learning and are not able to prepare complete study materials. Just as absences and lateness can doom you in the workplace, they can doom you in the classroom as well.

3. BE Up Front!

If you were going to camp out for two days and nights so you could be among the first to purchase concert tickets to watch your favorite music group, when you got to the ticket window, which seats would you choose? Probably front row, center. There you could study how the musicians' fingers strum difficult licks and watch the sweat run down their foreheads. As for sound, you wouldn't miss a note. And, yet, where do students arriving early for class choose to sit? They grab the seats in the rear of the classroom or along the sides—places with lots of distractions, places where they can't see or hear well.

Sit toward the front of the classroom, where it's easier to focus attention. If you sit toward the back, there are more potential distractions between you and the instructor. As students in front of you shift in their seats, tap their pens, or swing their crossed legs, your attention is drawn to their sounds and movements. The back of the room is also where slackers tend to sit, so they can carry on conversations with and whisper comments to one another. The instructor might not notice them, but if you're sitting nearby, you will.

When you sit toward the front, you get the feeling that the instructor is actually talking to you. Your attention is focused on what the instructor is saying, and you're more likely to take complete notes. Serious students and concertgoers know the best place to sit: front and center.

4. BE on the Edge!

Olympic skiers ski on the edge. Top students are on the edge too—the edge of their seats.

It does no good to go to class early, grab a front-row seat, and then sit passively throughout the lecture like a zombie. Instead, you should be right on the edge of your seat, as if you were watching the final, heart-wrenching scene in *Romeo and Juliet*. Lean into the lecture as if you were trying to hear Romeo's dying words. Follow the instructor as intently as if he were Friar Laurence eulogizing the dead lovers. Don't miss a word. Be prepared emotionally, physically, and mentally.

Prepare emotionally. Some students sabotage their academic success and lecture learning by dampening their mood and motivation before lectures begin. They simply show up for lectures in hopes that instructors will fill their minds with knowledge the way bakers fill a cake mold. Consequently, during lectures they daydream and only occasionally tune in—as if they were watching an old movie. Later, they complain that they can't learn because the instructor is boring.

Now consider Tom, who worked at the University of Nebraska's Academic Success Center. Students often came there in a zombie-like state complaining that they couldn't learn from lectures because their instructor was boring and caused them to fall asleep or daydream. Upon request, these students showed Tom their lecture notes, which were often as barren as a rain gauge in Arizona. Tom told them that he would attend their next class and meet them afterward.

Tom attended that next lecture emotionally "pumped up" for learning even though the subject was outside his area. His sole mission was to learn and record every important idea uttered. Tom got there early and sat in the front row on the edge of his seat. He wrote feverishly, pausing only to ask a question, seek a clarification, voice a comment, or wipe the sweat from his brow. He didn't daydream. He was completely engaged in the lecture. He loved it. During the break, he followed the instructor to the restroom and asked more about the field. Before class resumed, Tom started the paperwork for switching his major. Not really . . . but he was excited by what he was learning. After the lecture, Tom met the complaining students and they compared notes. The students had each recorded half a page of notes, and one of them said, "See, isn't this stuff boring?" Tom, meanwhile, had recorded eight pages of notes and was brimming with excitement and still red faced from his effort. They had attended the same lecture. The students, however, chose to be emotionally flat; Tom chose to be emotionally pumped up. Which will you choose? The choice is yours.

Prepare physically. It's important to maintain concentration throughout a lecture. It's common for students to take fewer notes in the second half of lectures because they tire, lean back in their seats, and begin to listen for the final bell. Stave off fatigue by being in top physical condition. Get plenty of sleep, exercise regularly, and go to class neither too hungry nor too full to concentrate. Also, be physically ready by having all necessary materials on hand.

We've all mistakenly failed to have things we needed. Ever forget to pack matches for a camping trip, neglect to take a water bottle along on a long bike ride, or fail to have enough toilet paper on hand? Good forethought could have avoided these oversights. Have the right materials on hand for lecture learning. You should have a separate notebook for each subject. A three-ring binder is probably the best, because you can easily add and remove pages. Handouts tucked inside a spiral notebook usually fall out and are either misplaced or lost.

Clearly mark each notebook's subject on the cover so that you don't carry the wrong notebook to class. Notebooks should also include your name, address, and telephone number on the inside cover, in the event that they are left behind, temporarily appropriated by a foreign agent, or abducted and held for ransom.

Come to lectures equipped with an arsenal of working pens and pencils. Don't be like Lanny at the beginning of the chapter, whose only pen was dry and whose only pencil was worn to an eraserless nub.

Have the class textbook and handouts available at lectures, too. Occasionally, instructors refer to diagrams, graphs, or assignments found in the text, or follow course outlines or objectives they provided earlier.

Finally, have available any special tools or materials appropriate to the class. Your math instructor, for example, may suggest that you bring a calculator to class.

In your design class, special drawing instruments and sketch pads might be necessary. Have your notebook and other materials on your desk and ready to go before the lecture.

Prepare mentally. Let's face it. Lecture learning is a brain drain because lectures are usually delivered at top speed, lack organization, and contain unfamiliar information. Prepare your brain for lectures by reviewing previous notes and by reading related text chapters ahead of time. These activities help compensate for speedy lectures because they can be carried out at your own pace. You have all the time in the world to review notes and read text material. These prelecture activities are also likely to reveal how the lecture information is best organized. When you read the psychology chapter about schedules of reinforcement in advance of the lecture, for example, you learn that the schedules are organized by whether they are interval or ratio and whether they are fixed or variable. This information helps you to organize your eventual lecture notes and understand associations among the lecture ideas. Finally, prelecture activities supply background knowledge or hooks for grasping the lecture ideas. For instance, the text might indicate that schedules of reinforcement are often used to train circus animals and to control behavior in prisons. This background knowledge helps you to relate lecture ideas to familiar contexts and gain a deeper understanding of the lecture material.

Don't go into a lecture mentally unprepared. The lecturer is going to strap on the crash helmet and push the pedal to the metal. The degree to which you are able to follow along depends entirely on your level of understanding going in. If the gap between your knowledge and the lecturer's starting point is too great, you'll be left behind in a puff of smoke. Read, review, and be ready to roll.

During the Lecture

During the lecture, you want to record complete notes. To be sure you do, don't forget the "Four GETS"—GET it all, GET it fast, GET it now, and GET it again.

1. GET It All!

Many students record only the information they do not understand. When they later review, all they have to study is a bunch of information they still don't understand. Others just jot down the main ideas. They leave out all the details, hoping that the main ideas will help them recall the details. But unless the details are recorded, they won't be recalled. Still other students record main ideas and details—but then leave out examples. As soon as the lecturer begins a "story" or example, many students drop their pens, lean back in their seats, and enjoy the stories and examples, which they believe are just incidental to the lecture. But, in fact, examples are crucial for fully understanding new concepts and for good performance on example questions.

To illustrate the interplay among and importance of main ideas, details, and examples, suppose your psychology instructor reported that short-term memory has a limited capacity. You should select and note this *main idea*. The instructor then mentions that short-term memory has a capacity of approximately seven bits of information. You should select and note this *detail*. The lecturer then remarks that telephone numbers and zip codes were developed not to exceed the capacity of short-term memory. You should select and note these *examples*. The resulting notes might look like this:

Short-term memory (STM) = limited capacity

- 7 bits
- Ex: telephone #s
           zip codes

The purpose of note taking is to record a complete account of the lecture. From your notes, you should be able to re-create the lecture months later. This is not to suggest that you should record the lecturer's every word. Doing so is mindless and fails to select the key lecture ideas. Instead, you should select and record all the main ideas, details, and examples presented and write these in your own words. Although these notes need not be recorded in sentence form, they should be recorded completely enough so that you can understand them later, as shown in the sample notes for short-term memory. Notice that phrases, symbols, and abbreviations are used, rather than complete sentences.

What follows is a portion of a lecture on creativity. Try recording a complete set of notes that contains main ideas, details, and examples. Then examine the notes I prepared and compare them with yours.

Creativity

Expressive creativity is defined as the ability to make a quick, or a series of very quick, responses in a situation. The time necessary to produce the creative response is only a few seconds. Examples include a soccer player changing her dribble to beat her opponent, an actor improvising in the theater, or a comedian reacting to an audience. In each case, the person makes a series of responses that appear spontaneous or unrehearsed. In actuality, the expressively creative person has made a very similar response in very similar situations before. Thus, an important characteristic is the ability to see very rapidly how a new situation is similar to an old situation. Returning to the example of the comedian, a heckler in the audience might "put down" the comedian. The comedian, however, seeing the

> relationship between what this heckler has said and previous situations involving hecklers, is able to "put down" or respond to the heckler quickly. The time necessary to develop this sort of creativity is usually 8–12 years. Another characteristic associated with expressive creativity is timing. The person has to learn when to make the responses.

My notes on this lecture look like the ones in Exhibit 2.1. They contain the main idea (definition), details (such as time to respond, responses, characteristics, and time to develop), and examples that are paraphrased rather than word for word. The notes are brief but complete enough to reconstruct the lecture. They also contain abbreviations, which are helpful for quickly recording a complete set of notes.

To help you get all the important lecture information, pay special attention to the lecture cues. My own research shows that clear lecture cues can easily double student note taking. In one study, a group listening to an uncued lecture recorded about 40 percent of the lecture ideas, whereas students listening to a cued lecture recorded about 80 percent of the lecture ideas. Naturally, the cued group performed much better than the uncued group on a test of the entire lecture.

Lecturers use many cues to signal important ideas. It is crucial that you record these highlighted ideas in notes, and mark them with an asterisk or some other symbol that signals their importance. Cues can be nonverbal, spoken, or written.

EXHIBIT 2.1   Lecture notes.

CREATIVITY

Expressive
Def—making very quick response(s)
Time to respond—few s.
Ex—soccer player changing dribble
    actor improvising
    comedian reacting
Responses—appear spontaneous, unrehearsed, actually similar response to similar situation
Characteristic—see rapidly how two situations are alike
Ex—comedian's response to heckler seems spontaneous but is similar to other responses to other hecklers
Time to develop—8–12 yrs
Characteristic—timing, when to make response

Exercise 1

Below is another portion of a lecture. Construct a set of lecture notes. Indicate whether each note is a main idea, a detail, or an example.

> To the human eye, stars seem to be about the same size. In truth, many stars are larger than our sun. They appear small because of their great distance.
>
> Stars seem to vary in brightness. This is due to their distance, size, or temperature. A very large star such as Sirius, the Dog Star, appears bright because it is close and very hot. The star Vega, in the Harp constellation, is three times farther away from Earth than Sirius but appears just as bright because of its extreme heat. Rigel, in the constellation Orion, is 540 light-years from Earth, but because it is very large and very hot, it appears as one of the brightest stars. In the same constellation, the star Betelgeuse is only 270 light-years away, and although not as hot as Rigel, it appears nearly as bright. This is because of its immense size.

One college instructor I had emphasized important points nonverbally by resting his chin in his hand, jutting out his bottom lip, arching his eyebrows, and nodding his head vehemently. His students were alert for this cue and wrote feverishly when they saw it. Other nonverbal cues might include pointing; clapping; finger snapping; hand waving; a piercing glance; an extended pause; or variations in voice pitch, volume, cadence, or speed.

Spoken cues can signal importance, such as when an instructor says that a point is "noteworthy," "critical," "important," or "imperative." The not-too-subtle phrase "This will be on your test," of course, should not be overlooked. When an instructor repeats a term or phrase, this also signals importance. Be sure to note this important information along with an asterisk or other symbol to indicate its importance.

Written cues are those that appear on a chalkboard, an overhead, a PowerPoint slide, or a handout. Take special note of these. If instructors bother to write this information, you can bet it's really important. Most students are well aware of the importance of chalkboard information. I have observed many students recording the scribbles left behind from the classroom's previous

Be alert to lecture cues!

lecturer, who forgot to erase the board. When instructors prepare written outlines, questions, or objectives, make detailed notes related to these lecture aids. These written aids are provided to signal important ideas and guide note taking.

2. GET It Fast!

Besides taking notes using phrases rather than full sentences, compensate for rapid lecture rates by using abbreviations and notations while recording lecture notes. Some common abbreviations and their translations are listed in Exhibit 2.2.

Probably the most useful abbreviations are those you construct within a unit of instruction. For example, in a unit on behavioral psychology, you might use the abbreviations in Exhibit 2.3. Be certain to write the term in full along with its abbreviation (e.g., positive reinforcement [PR]) the first time so that you will know what the abbreviation means when studying your notes later.

EXHIBIT 2.2   *Some common note-taking abbreviations.*

Abbreviation	Translation
cf.	compare
e.g.	for example
ex.	for example
etc.	and so forth
i.e.	that is
vs	versus
et al.	and others
w/out	without
cm	centimeter
s	second
min	minute
lb	pound
ft	foot
Mon	Monday
05	2005

EXHIBIT 2.3   *Abbreviations developed for a unit on behavioral psychology.*

BP	Behavioral Psychology	S	Stimulus
PR	Positive Reinforcement	R	Response
NR	Negative Reinforcement	FI	Fixed Interval
PP	Positive Punishment	VI	Variable Interval
NP	Negative Punishment	FR	Fixed Ratio
EX	Extinction	VR	Variable Ratio

Certain notations or symbols are useful, too. Some common ones are shown in Exhibit 2.4.

EXHIBIT 2.4   *Common notations for note taking.*

Notation	Translation
Ψ	Psychology
=	Equal to
≈	Approximately
∴	Therefore
↑	Increase
→	Leads to
#	Number
1, 2, 3 . . .	Lists

Exercise 2

Make a list of other common abbreviations and notations you might use when recording lecture notes for the courses you are taking.

3. GET It Now!

Suppose you are at a raffle and the prize is a $1,000 mountain bike. The raffler draws a slip of paper from a large barrel and reads the eight-digit winning number over the public-address system. The quality of the system is terrible, due to low volume and a crackling noise, so the numbers are barely audible. You decipher a few numbers that match those on your ticket. No one steps forward to claim the prize. What do you do?

The solution is obvious. You ask the raffler to repeat the numbers. The possible consequence of mishearing the numbers is too severe to take the chance of not hearing them again.

But students attending lectures rarely ask instructors to repeat information they do not hear clearly—information that is critically important to understanding the lecture. Students rarely take steps to make sure they get valuable information before it's too late. I did one time see a superb example of a "student" being sure she got what she came for. I was attending a national convention and was one of about 1,000 conference registrants listening to a panel speak about the topic of expertise. One speaker was not using the microphone effectively and his voice was occasionally inaudible. A woman seated in the back row of this jam-packed room stood on her chair and screamed, "Please use the microphone!" Hooray for her. She didn't pay all that money and travel all that way to waste her time catching only an occasional syllable.

Assert yourself in lecture settings. Be polite, but forceful. If the instructor speaks too rapidly or too quietly, for example, ask the instructor to repeat the information. If there's information you don't understand, ask the instructor to clarify it by rephrasing or explaining it. Better yet, ask the instructor a question about the information. For example, "You mentioned that this related to reinforcement theory. Could you explain how?"

What do you do when the instructor is displaying a detailed slide or an overhead on a screen and continues to lecture, as was the case during Lanny's lecture? Do you record the lecturer's words or pay attention to the visual display? Assert yourself now by asking for a quiet moment to record notes about the visual display. If the instructor doesn't stop lecturing, then record the spoken lecture in notes (because spoken words are fleeting). After class, ask to see the display and take notes on it then.

Remember that successful lecture learning depends on recording complete notes. Treat all lecture information as if it could be your winning number in a lottery. If you don't exercise some responsibility in how the lecture is delivered, you are going to pay the consequences of missing valuable information.

4. GET It Again!

If at first you don't succeed, repeat the lecture again.

Perhaps you're following the tips for complete note taking described here and still record notes that are relatively incomplete. Incomplete note taking might result from the lecture being presented rapidly, containing too many noteworthy details, or being poorly organized. In any event, there is something else that you can do during the lecture to ensure that you have complete notes later.

When it is difficult to record complete notes, tape-record (or videotape) the lecture and play it back one or more times following the lecture. As you replay the lecture, add to your existing set of notes. My own research shows that doing so helps you record more notes—particularly details—and recall more lecture points than if you hear a lecture only once and record only a single set of notes. The first time you hear a lecture, you are likely to note the lecturer's main ideas but miss many important details and examples. These are easily added to your notes when you hear or see the lecture again.

After the Lecture

Remember that most students are notoriously incomplete note takers, recording, on average, about 40 percent of the important lecture content. Using the "BE" (for before the lecture) and "GET" (for during the lecture) techniques taught in this chapter should greatly increase and improve your note taking. Still, it's likely that while recording lecture notes you'll note a few things incorrectly and omit some key ideas. Therefore, continue to improve notes after the lecture by "upping" the number of correctly noted ideas. To do so, fill UP and fix UP.

Fill UP and Fix UP!

Take a few minutes following the lecture, preferably that same day, while the material is still fresh in your mind, and read your notes thoughtfully. While doing so, seek to fix any incorrect statements and to fill in any missing information—particularly details and examples—because these were more likely omitted. My own informal research with students shows that this revision process commonly adds another 20 percent of lecture information to notes. Students originally noting 40 percent of lecture ideas, for example, usually extend their notes to include about 60 percent of lecture ideas. This increase occurs because the original notes serve as prompts for remembering related lecture ideas that were not noted. For instance, your notes might include the statement "Short-term memory is limited." That notation might, in turn, remind you of other related ideas that the lecturer reported, namely, that short-term memory is limited to seven bits of information and that many numbers, such as zip codes and phone numbers, contain seven or fewer digits so as not to exceed short-term memory limitations. Having recalled these "new" ideas, you simply add them to your lecture notes.

Work with classmates after the lecture to fill up and fix up notes.

Exercise 3

Return to some lecture notes you recently recorded. Try to fill up and fix up your notes. Confer with a study partner if possible to facilitate your postlecture note taking.

To improve notes even more, meet with a few students from the class sometime during the next few days after the lecture. You and your fellow students should take turns reading portions of your notes aloud. Group members should add missing points to their notes and offer noted points to help others complete their notes. My students have used this technique and have increased their notes so that they contain about 80 percent of the important lecture ideas! If your group is still missing lecture information after you meet, ask your instructor to help you fill in the gaps.

During group sessions, you can also fix up your notes. For instance, you might occasionally record misinformation during the lecture in your haste to record complete notes. You might, for example, note during a psychology lecture that proactive interference is interference occurring *after* other material is learned. Actually, proactive interference is interference occurring *before* other material is learned. It's an easy mistake to make, and the group session is the perfect place to find the error and make the correction.

Exercise 4

Complete the following matrix showing strategies or tips for effective note taking:

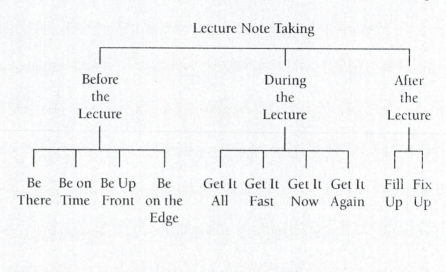

Lecture Note Taking

Before the Lecture — During the Lecture — After the Lecture

Be There Be on Time Be Up Front Be on the Edge   Get It All Get It Fast Get It Now Get It Again   Fill Up Fix Up

Strategies:

And, one more thing: Don't look a gift horse in the mouth (although I'm not sure where you're supposed to look at it). If your instructor gives you notes to review, like Dr. Fletcher did, certainly make good use of them. The instructor has selected and noted the vital information for you.

SELECTING AND NOTING TEXT INFORMATION

Although lectures and texts might say the same thing, they are different animals. Lectures are fleeting and demanding; texts are permanent and flexible. Lectures demand that you be in a certain place, at a certain time, and gather the rapidly presented information quickly. Texts, on the other hand, are read anywhere, anytime, and at your own pace.

Whether you are learning from lecture or text, if you're going to SOAR to success, you must first select ideas for further study. Let's examine now how that is best done for text learning.

Most students select text ideas by highlighting them within the text. They do this either by underlining the information with a pen or by highlighting it with a colored marker. There are three problems associated with highlighting:

Problem 1. Students tend to highlight too much information. Have you bought a used textbook lately and noticed how some pages look like they were spray painted yellow? Students often mindlessly highlight nearly everything, believing that highlighting equals understanding. This results in a marked text where the nonhighlighted information actually stands out more than the highlighted portions.

Problem 2. The activity of highlighting alone is not effective. Students who highlight while they read do not remember their highlighted ideas any better than students who read the same text without highlighting it.

Problem 3. When students later study their highlighted text, they remember their highlighted ideas better than students who study their nonhighlighted text—but at a cost. Those who highlighted do not remember nonhighlighted portions well, and they tend to learn highlighted ideas in a piecemeal fashion. They have trouble grasping the overall meaning of the text or understanding how text ideas relate to each other.

If highlighting is not the ticket, then what should students do to select text information for further study? The answer is a familiar one. Just as is true for lecture note taking, readers should record complete notes that contain main ideas, details, and examples. Moreover, readers should be certain to paraphrase their notes rather than copy sentences verbatim from the text. Recording paraphrased notes is important because it prevents you from mindlessly copying ideas. Paraphrasing forces you to think about and understand the material before recording it.

It probably doesn't matter whether you record text notes on paper or in the text's margin just as long as the margin provides ample space to record complete notes containing main ideas, details, and examples. Following is a brief passage about memory. Exhibit 2.5 is a set of text notes for the passage.

Memory

Psychologists believe there are three different types of memory stores: sensory, short term, and long term. Sensory memory has a large capacity. It holds all the sights, sounds, and other sensations in the environment. It holds all these things for just a second or so to allow you time to decide what to pay attention to. While your attention is focused on the pitcher at a ball game, all other sensations—crowd noise, the smell of popcorn, a bird flying overhead—are briefly recorded in your sensory memory to allow you time to consider them quickly and perhaps shift attention. You quickly forget all the information in sensory memory, though, as it is pushed out by new incoming information.

Short-term memory has a brief duration too: 15–20 seconds. It also has a limited capacity. It only holds about seven things at a time. Short-term memory is like a workbench. It can't hold a lot of things but whatever you're working on at the time—or thinking about—is present in short-term memory. Forgetting occurs when old information fades or is pushed out by new information entering short-term memory.

Long-term memory is indeed long. Some believe its duration is infinite and that people never truly forget. Forgetting occurs because people simply can't locate the "missing" information stored in long-term memory. Regarding capacity, long-term memory has no limits. It can store more than any computer. If short-term memory is the workbench, then long-term memory is the shelves used to store all the tools and supplies.

EXHIBIT 2.5   *Notes on memory.*

3 types of memory
    Sensory (S)
    Short term (STM)
    Long term (LTM)

S
    Capacity—large
        all input from senses
    Duration—sec or so
    Purpose—provides time to consider stimuli and shift attention
    Ex.—Focus on baseball pitcher but other stimuli in envir. (noise, smells)
    recorded in S
    Forgetting—new info pushes out old

STM
    Duration—brief
        15–20 sec
    Capacity—limited
        ≈7 items
    Ex.—workbench
        Holds only a few items
        What you are working on (thinking about)
    Forgetting—info fades
        Info displaced

LTM
    Duration—infinite
    Forgetting—none or can't locate it
    Capacity—no limit
        More than computer
    Ex.—storage shelves around workbench

Exercise 5

Record a set of notes from the passage below.

Running and Swimming

Running is an excellent activity for increasing one's level of physical conditioning. It increases aerobic capacity (which is the ability to turn oxygen into energy) and uses many muscle systems in the body. It is especially good for strengthening the legs. Running can be done almost anywhere and in almost all weather conditions. Therefore, when people travel for vacation or business, running is easy to continue. The only special equipment required is a good pair of running shoes to support the arches of the feet. The main disadvantage of running is that it is somewhat taxing on the joints of the ankles, knees, and hips. Another disadvantage is that running decreases flexibility.

Swimming is considered the best overall body conditioner. It increases aerobic capacity and exercises almost all of the major muscle systems in the body. It is especially good for strengthening the upper body and for increasing flexibility. Swimming can be done indoors in a pool or outdoors in a pool or a lake or other body of water. Many people swim year round, even when the water is cold. Swimming requires a comfortable swimsuit and a pair of watertight goggles. The disadvantages of swimming are that one must have access to a pool or a lake or other body of water, and many people feel that it does not control weight as well as other forms of exercise.

SUMMARY

Studying for tests depends first on selecting key ideas and recording a complete set of notes to review. Unfortunately, students are notoriously poor note takers. They record only about 40 percent of the points covered in a lecture even though they stand only a 5 percent chance of later recalling a nonnoted idea. You can do several things to make notes more complete.

Before a lecture, do the four BEs:

1. BE There! If you don't attend lectures you'll have nothing to review.

2. BE on Time! If you're late, you're missing valuable lecture information.

3. BE Up Front! Sit up front where there are fewer distractions and where it's easier to concentrate.

4. BE on the Edge! Be prepared emotionally, like Tom, pumped up to record all the key lecture ideas. Be prepared physically by having the necessary materials on hand and being in good physical shape come lecture time. Be prepared mentally by reading related text chapters and reviewing previous notes before lectures.

During lectures, GET with it!

1. GET It All! Record all main ideas, details, and examples. Follow the lecturer's cues as to what's particularly important.

2. GET It Fast! Jot down phrases rather than complete sentences and use abbreviations and notations to speed note taking.

3. GET It Now! Slow down fast-talking lecturers by raising questions, offering comments, or simply asking the lecturer to slow down or provide more note-taking time.

4. GET It Again! Tape-record or videotape lectures. Add to your notes when you replay the lecture later.

After lectures, UP the number of ideas in notes by filling UP and fixing UP notes. Seek to correct notes and make them more complete by rereading your notes alone and in groups.

When learning from text, do not carry out mindless highlighting activities like many students. Instead, record a complete set of notes on paper or in the text margin that capture main ideas, details, and examples.

Do all this and you will select and record all the important ideas needed to SOAR to success.

ANSWERS TO FOCUS QUESTIONS

1. Note taking is important because it helps you focus attention during lectures and it produces notes for further study.

2. Most students are incomplete note takers, recording only about 40 percent of important lecture ideas.

3. Before lectures, students should do the four BEs: BE there, BE on time, BE up front (sit toward the front of the classroom), and BE on the edge (of their seats straining to pay full attention to the lecture).

4. Prepare physically by being in top shape for lectures—well exercised, fed, and rested—and having all necessary materials on hand. Prepare mentally for lectures by reviewing previous notes and reading about the topic in advance. Prepare emotionally by being pumped up—in the mood—for lecture learning.

5. GET it all   C, E

   GET it fast   A

   GET it now   B

   GET it again   D

6. Fill UP and fix UP notes by going over them following the lecture. Try to add more notes (fill UP) and correct existing notes (fix UP). Doing this with other students makes notes even more complete.

7. Highlighting text information is problematic because (a) students are not selective and highlight too much information, (b) the process of highlighting does not improve retention of highlighted material, and (c) studying highlighted material often leads to piecemeal learning; students learn the highlighted facts but fail to learn nonhighlighted material, relate the highlighted facts, or grasp the text's larger meaning.

Organize Information

3

Overview

Focus Questions

1. Why does studying a matrix produce greater learning than studying an outline?

2. Match the four representation names on the left with the patterns on the right:

  1. Hierarchy   a.

  2. Sequence   b.

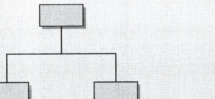

  3. Matrix   c.

  4. Illustration   d.

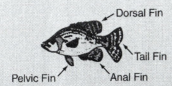

Dorsal Fin

Tail Fin

Pelvic Fin   Anal Fin

41

3. Match the four representation names on the left with the type of relationship it represents:

   1. Hierarchy   a. Comparative

   2. Sequence   b. Positional

   3. Matrix   c. Time

   4. Illustration   d. Set–Subset

4. In the representation below, what is the subset of C?

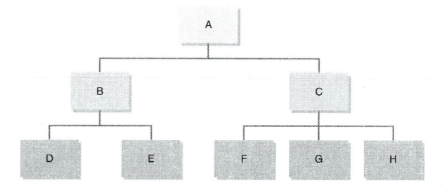

5. Given the following sentences, identify the alert word and construct a preliminary representation of the content for each:

   A. There are three types of cancer.

   B. The embryo turns into a fetus.

   C. There are similarities between Republicans and Democrats.

   D. Jessie is next to Marie.

6. What is wrong with the representation below? See if you can improve it.

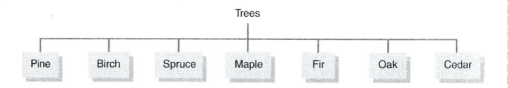

7. Extend the representations below to create a matrix framework:

   A. Phases of the Moon

   B.

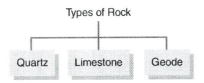

   C.

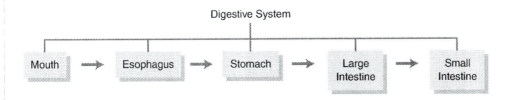

8. Improve the matrix below:

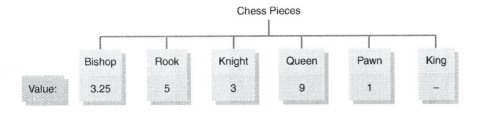

9. What are three tips for constructing illustrations?

10. Construct simple multiple representations pertaining to the topic of corrective vision.

Keth: Sandy, I studied for the psychology quiz. I tried to memorize these definitions of operant concepts but I couldn't keep them straight.

> *Operant Concepts*
> - *Positive reinforcement:* A stimulus is presented following a behavior and the behavior increases.
> - *Negative reinforcement:* A stimulus is removed following a behavior and the behavior increases.
> - *Positive punishment:* A stimulus is presented following a behavior and the behavior decreases.
> - *Negative punishment:* A stimulus is removed following a behavior and the behavior decreases.

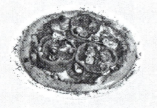

Keth: Can you help me?

Sandy: What's in it for me?

Keth: If you can teach me how to learn this stuff, I'll treat you to a mushroom and garlic pie at the Factory.

Sandy: Ah, the magic words! Throw in pepperoni, oh Swami, and you've got a deal.

Keth: What choice do I have! I'm just a thin crust from failing. Pepperoni it is. Now work your magic.

Sandy: The key, Keth, is learning the concepts all together.

Keth: Say what?

Sandy: These four concepts are related. To understand them, they have to be tossed together like the vegetables in a salad.

Keth: No upping the ante, Sandy. I promised pizza, not salad.

Sandy: I was speaking figuratively. Lettuce continue, oh tomato head. Look at the names of the first two concepts: positive reinforcement and negative reinforcement. Do you think they are alike in some way?

Keth: I suppose. They're both a type of reinforcement.

Sandy: Right. Do you think they are different in some way?

Keth: I suppose.

Sandy: They must be, otherwise there would be just one concept called "reinforcement." Your job is to find out how they're alike and how they're different. Read the definitions and find out.

Keth: They're alike because they both *increase* behavior. They're different because positive reinforcement involves a *presented* stimulus and negative reinforcement involves a *removed* stimulus.

Sandy: Way to go! I can smell that pizza baking. Now, without reading the definitions, predict how punishment differs from reinforcement.

Keth: Well, if reinforcement involves an increase in behavior, I predict that punishment means a decrease.

Sandy: Okay. What is your prediction about positive and negative punishment based on what you learned about reinforcement?

Keth: My hunch is that positive punishment involves a *presented* stimulus and that negative punishment involves a *removed* stimulus. Am I warm?

Sandy: Like a pizza oven.

Keth: Wow! I knew the definitions before I even read them! This is magic!

Sandy: It gets better, oh pizza supplier.

Keth: Now do I have to kick in the salad?

Sandy: Save your croutons. I'll show you how to organize this information using a representation so you can see all the relationships at once and be able to remember the concepts easily. Look at this matrix representation I developed. When you read it vertically, it shows that when a behavior increases, reinforcement has occurred, and when a behavior decreases, punishment has occurred. When you read it horizontally, it shows that when a stimulus is presented, the technique is positive, and when a stimulus is removed, the technique is negative.

Operant Concepts

Behavior

	Increase	Decrease
Presented	Positive Reinforcement	Positive Punishment
Removed	Negative Reinforcement	Negative Punishment

Stimulus

Keth: This matrix organization is awesome for seeing relationships. This operant concept stuff is easy.

Sandy: As easy as pie.

Suppose your biology instructor wants to teach you about human bones. To help you learn, he places a replica of each bone in the human skeleton in a long line across the floor. You examine each bone in turn and study it carefully. Is this organization of bones helpful?

Not really. Although this organization might help you observe how bones vary somewhat in shape or size, it doesn't teach you how the bones join together to form a hand, ribcage, or complete skeleton. Examining each bone separately is about as helpful as examining a jigsaw puzzle that's lying in separate pieces on the floor. The scattered pieces don't provide much hint of what the assembled puzzle will look like.

Unfortunately, information is usually presented to you, and recorded in your notes, in a linear form, one idea at a time, like puzzle pieces strewn across a floor. This is true when an instructor speaks the information in a lecture, or when you see it printed in a paragraph, an outline, or a list. The fact is that schools have fed you a steady diet of linear information, which has made it difficult for you to learn relationships among those "pieces" of information.

You might protest that if that's true, then teachers and textbook authors should present information in nonlinear ways to aid learning. Some do, but many do not. When they present information in linear ways, *you* must convert linear presentations into an organized set of notes that highlight, rather than obscure, relationships.

Effective learners learn in spite of poor instruction. They do not excuse themselves from learning because information is poorly organized. Don't be content to examine each "bone" or "puzzle piece" separately when you can assemble the entire "skeleton" or "puzzle." The piecemeal approach to learning is the costliest educational mistake that you can make, because examining information one piece at a time increases your study time and prevents you from learning the relationships among those pieces.

To demonstrate that the piecemeal approach is ineffective, consider the following example: Suppose you're studying whales in a marine biology course. Your instructor lectures about two small whales: dolphins and porpoises. The instructor provides three important facts about dolphins: they are about 12 feet long, have beaklike snouts, and swim far from shore. Later, your instructor describes porpoises and explains that they are about 6 feet long; have short, blunt snouts; and swim near shore. Certainly, you can learn each of the six facts separately, but doing so causes problems.

One problem is that the pieces are never assembled to reveal the "big picture"—the relationships among the pieces. Remember

Examining information in a piecemeal fashion does not reveal the full picture.

EXHIBIT 3.1   *Matrix representation comparing dolphins and porpoises.*

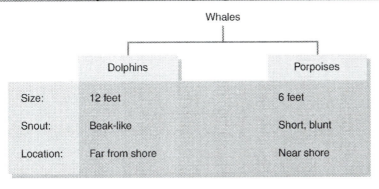

how the piecemeal approach obscured the "human skeleton" and the completed "puzzle." Now, examine Exhibit 3.1. The information about dolphins and porpoises is organized and represented in what's called a matrix. The matrix helps you see the big picture. As you read down and across the matrix, notice that a revealing picture comes into focus—the dolphin is "greater" than the porpoise in all respects. The dolphin is longer, has a longer snout, and swims farther from shore. Recognizing this pattern makes learning more meaningful. It makes sense that a larger animal has a longer snout and lives in deeper, more remote waters. The individual ideas alone do not produce this meaningful revelation.

A second problem associated with the piecemeal approach is that because facts are learned one at a time, learning time is increased. Isn't it harder to figure out what the whole picture will be from looking at each puzzle piece instead of looking at the single picture emerging from the completed puzzle? Recognizing patterns reduces learning time because you learn facts collectively. Where dolphins and porpoises are concerned, the easy and quick thing to remember is that everything about the dolphin is greater.

To summarize, learning depends on organizing ideas so that relationships and patterns are apparent. Collections of individual bones or puzzle pieces reveal little about the human skeleton or the completed puzzle. The piecemeal approach to learning must be replaced with an organized approach showing how ideas are connected.

This chapter shows you how to organize information by constructing what are called representations—like those for schedules of reinforcement, operant concepts, and whales. Representations display information in organized but nonlinear ways. Paragraphs, outlines, and lists are examples of information presented in linear ways. Representations include things such as charts (matrices) and illustrations that are nonlinear and help you to associate represented ideas and learn relationships.

To SOAR to success, you need to organize the ideas you've selected. Representations help you do this. In this chapter you'll learn more about why you should use representations, what representations to use, and how to construct them.

Exercise 1

Try to solve this problem in two minutes. Hint: A piecemeal approach will not work. You'll need to organize the information into a matrix.

The Mr. Young Problem

1. The man with asthma is in room 101.
2. Mr. Alex has cancer.
3. Mr. Osborne is in room 105.
4. Mr. Wilson has TB.
5. The man with mono is in room 104.
6. Mr. Thomas is in room 101.
7. Mr. Wilson is in room 102.
8. One of the men has epilepsy.
9. One of the patients is in room 103.

What disease does Mr. Young have?

WHY USE REPRESENTATIONS?

My research shows that studying representations improves learning over studying the same information organized in paragraph, outline, or list form. The main reason is that paragraphs, outlines, and lists are linear—they present separate pieces one after another—and therefore often hide relationships that representations accent. Exhibit 3.2 is an outline of information about moths and butterflies. Let's compare it with the matrix representation in Exhibit 3.3.

Right away you notice that the matrix is two dimensional. It can therefore be read vertically (first moths then butterflies) like the outline, but it can also be read horizontally along its common categories, such as development, wings, rest, and antennae. Reading the matrix horizontally makes it easy to compare moths and butterflies along common categories. Information about the insects' antennae, for example, is in the same matrix row but is separated by six lines in the outline. Obviously, when related information is closer together it is easier to compare. Now, suppose the outline and matrix reported on six insects instead of two. Information about antennae would appear in six different parts of the outline but in a single matrix row—again making comparison easier with the matrix.

Look again at the matrix in Exhibit 3.3. Notice how easy it is to make internal associations among ideas. Immediately, you see that moths and butterflies are alike in their development and wings. You see that there is missing information about the butterflies' cocoon but not the moths'. Moreover, by comparing the insects' differences, it is apparent that butterflies overall have more pronounced and showy characteristics than moths. Butterflies are brightly colored. They stretch out their colorful wings and display their odd antennae during daylight, when they can be

EXHIBIT 3.2   *Outline representation of moths and butterflies.*

Moths

- Wings—two sets
- Rest—wings folded down
- Antennae—feathery
- Cocoon—fuzzy
- Color—dull
- Flight—night
- Stages of development—egg, caterpillar, pupa, adult

Butterflies

- Wings—two sets
- Rest—wings outstretched
- Antennae—long and thin with knobs
- Color—bright
- Flight—day
- Stages of development—egg, caterpillar, pupa, adult

EXHIBIT 3.3   *Matrix representation of moths and butterflies.*

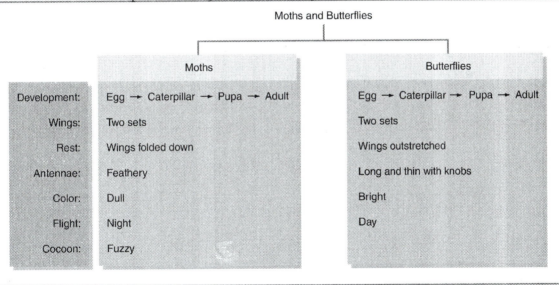

easily seen. Moths, by contrast, are dull colored. They hide their wings, have bland antennae, and are barely visible at night. These associations are harder to create from the outline because comparative information is separated.

In summary, you should use representations whenever possible because they organize information in ways that help you associate related information better than do paragraphs, outlines, or lists.

CONSTRUCTING REPRESENTATIONS

Representations show relationships. My colleague Nelson DuBois and I developed a simple representation system that includes four types of representations: hierarchy, sequence, matrix, and illustration. Each organizes information in a unique way and reveals a unique type of relationship. Now you'll meet each type of representation as well as learn what relationship it represents and tips for constructing it.

Hierarchy

A hierarchy organizes information in a top-to-bottom fashion to reveal hierarchical (or what can be called set–subset) relationships.

Exhibit 3.4 shows a hierarchy for types of birds. You'll notice, among other things, these hierarchical relationships: there are three sets of birds—raptors, waterbirds, and songbirds; three subsets of waterbirds—ducks, geese, and swans; and two subsets of swans—trumpeter and black.

When you think about it, you'll be amazed at how often information is organized hierarchically. Exhibits 3.5 and 3.6 provide a sampling. Exhibit 3.5 shows a punctuation hierarchy. There are two main types of punctuation: end of sentence and within sentence. There are subsets for each. End-of-sentence punctuation marks are period, question mark, and exclamation point. Within-sentence punctuation marks are comma, dash, colon, and semicolon. Exhibit 3.6 shows a set of clouds (cirrus, cumulus, and stratus) and their subsets. Other hierarchies might be constructed to show hierarchical relations among government agencies, military personnel, investment options, marine life, and types of numbers, to name a few.

Tips for Constructing Hierarchies

1. Always construct hierarchies top to bottom so that set–subset relationships are clear. Later, you'll see that this top-to-bottom form is useful for combining hierarchies with other representations.

EXHIBIT 3.4   Bird hierarchy.

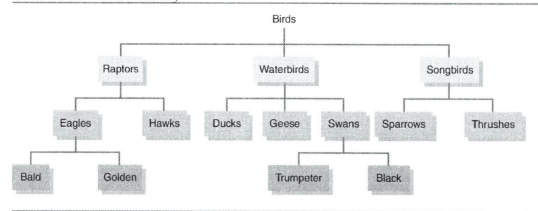

EXHIBIT 3.5   *Punctuation hierarchy.*

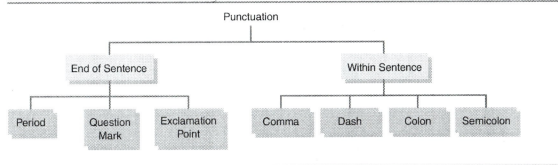

EXHIBIT 3.6   *Clouds hierarchy.*

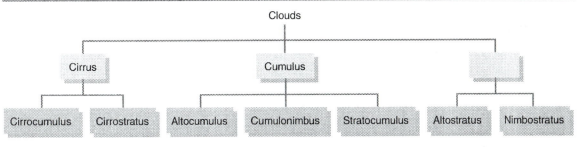

2. Be alert for certain words (alert words, I call them) telling you that information is organized hierarchically. When you hear or see these or similar words, creating a hierarchy is useful:

- parts
- types
- characteristics
- components
- elements
- kinds
- levels
- groups
- contain

Here are some examples of alert words and resulting hierarchies:

- The body's three main *parts* are the head, torso, and legs:

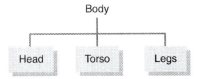

■ There are three *types* of food groups:

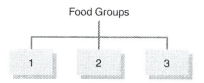

■ Atoms *contain* protons, electrons, and neutrons:

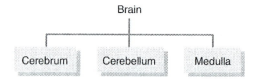

■ The brain has three *sections:* cerebrum, cerebellum, and medulla:

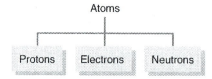

3. Include all levels. A hierarchy is more accurate and helpful when it displays all the important levels of information, as discussed next.

Exhibits 3.7 and 3.8 are poorly constructed hierarchies because they are missing important levels compared with their counterparts in Exhibits 3.9 and 3.10, respectively. Exhibit 3.7 is missing a level showing that some planets are inner

EXHIBIT 3.7   *Poorly constructed planet hierarchy.*

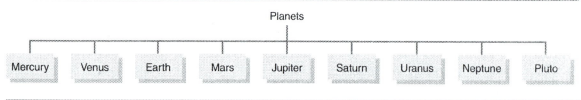

EXHIBIT 3.8   *Poorly constructed literature hierarchy.*

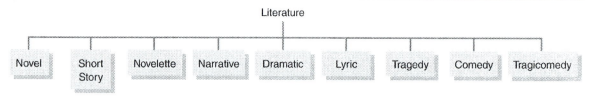

planets and others are outer planets. Exhibit 3.9 adds this important level to the hierarchy. Similarly, Exhibit 3.8 lumps all forms of literature into one big group. Exhibit 3.10 correctly groups these forms by adding a level to the hierarchy showing that literature is first divided into prose, poetry, and drama.

Tuck this little tidbit away: when you have seven or more things (planets, types of literature . . .), you probably don't. Often, these seven or more things can be better grouped after finding an important missing level in your hierarchy.

EXHIBIT 3.9   Well-constructed planet hierarchy.

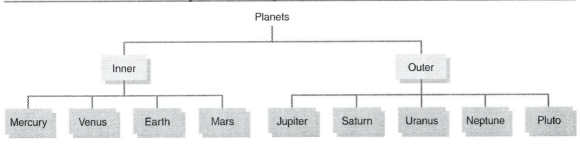

EXHIBIT 3.10   Well-constructed literature hierarchy.

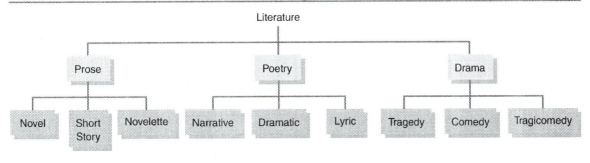

Exercise 2

1. Construct a hierarchy from the following list of foods:

cake	French fries
water	ice cream
potatoes	baked potatoes
pork chops	meats
prime rib	soda
beverages	desserts

2. Construct a hierarchy from the following biology terms:

liver	trachea
stomach	digestive system
esophagus	nostrils
respiratory system	excretory system
kidneys	skin
small intestine	

3. Construct two hierarchies from a course in your major.

Sequence

A sequence organizes information in a left-to-right fashion to reveal sequential (or time) relationships. Sequences show the order of things—what comes first, second, third, and so on—with arrows pointing left-to-right appearing between each step in the sequence.

Sequences appear in Exhibits 3.11–3.13. Exhibit 3.11 shows the steps in the scientific method. The scientist first raises a question, then plans the study, generates a hypothesis, conducts the study, and generates conclusions, all in that order.

Exhibits 3.12 and 3.13 show more complex sequences. Exhibit 3.12 (adding mixed fractions) shows how sequences can include subsequences. Notice, for example, that the step of changing mixed fractions to improper fractions actually includes the substeps of (1) multiplying the denominator by a whole number, (2) adding the numerator to the product, and (3) placing the sum over the denominator. Similarly, the step of producing fractions with common denominators includes the substeps numbered 4, 5, and 6. And the step for simplifying the fraction includes the substeps numbered 8 and 9. Exhibit 3.13 (experimental procedure) shows how sequences can be combined with hierarchies. Notice, for example, that the view lecture step contains a hierarchy below it showing the three ways that students might view the lecture: using conventional notes, a skeletal outline, or a matrix framework. Similarly, notice the hierarchy showing the three types of immediate tests: synthesis, application, and factual.

Much of what you learn can be represented sequentially. For example, the process of digestion, the plot in a story, historical events, the process of photosynthesis, the

EXHIBIT 3.11   A sequence displaying the scientific method.

Scientific Method

Raise Question ➡ Plan Study ➡ Generate Hypothesis ➡ Conduct Study ➡ Generate Conclusions

EXHIBIT 3.12   *Sequence and subsequences for adding mixed fractions.*

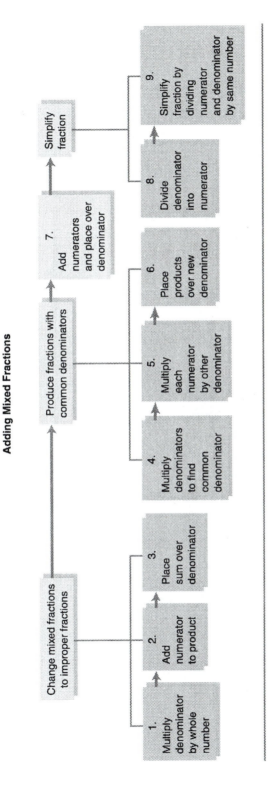

Adding Mixed Fractions

EXHIBIT 3.13   Sequence combined with hierarchies.

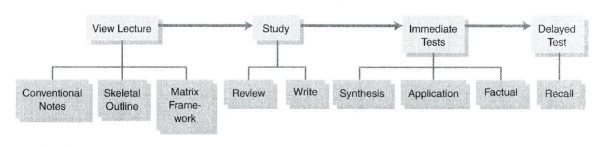

procedure for making coffee, trends in investments, the path of a storm, steps for programming a VCR, and the process for how brakes stop your car are all sequences.

Tips for Constructing Sequences

1. Always construct sequences left to right and place arrows between steps.
2. Be alert for certain alert words telling you that information is organized sequentially. When you see or hear these or similar words, construct a sequence representation:

- steps   - before
- stages   - develop
- phases   - first
- cycle   - later
- period   - causes
- next   - process

Here are some examples:

- Five *stages* of mitosis:

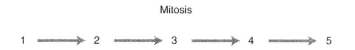

- In chess, you want to introduce knights *before* bishops:

■ *Development* of the embryo:

Development of the Embryo

■ The investment *trend* has gone from buying conservative bonds to buying volatile stocks to buying conservative stocks:

Investment Trends

Conservative Bonds ⟶ Volatile Stocks ⟶ Conservative Stocks

3. Include all levels. Just as hierarchies have levels, some sequences do too. Reexamine the sequence for adding mixed fractions in Exhibit 3.12. It could be represented as a single nine-step sequence. Learning nine steps, however, is confusing and difficult. Remember our maxim: If you have seven or more things, you probably don't. It is much simpler to think about and learn the process for adding mixed fractions as four major steps (with some steps containing substeps) than as nine steps.

Here's another example. Which sequence looks easier to remember? The one in Exhibit 3.14 or 3.15? Exhibit 3.15 is easier to remember, of course, because it organizes the 11 distinct steps shown in Exhibit 3.14 by showing how the steps fit within larger steps. You can see that there are three main steps: preexperimental, experimental, and postexperimental. Each, in turn, contains substeps. The postexperimental tasks, for instance, are the attitude survey and posttests. The posttests contain substeps too—fact, concept, and skill.

EXHIBIT 3.14 *Single-level sequence.*

Experimental Procedure

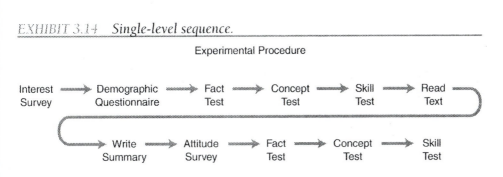

EXHIBIT 3.15   *Multilevel sequence.*

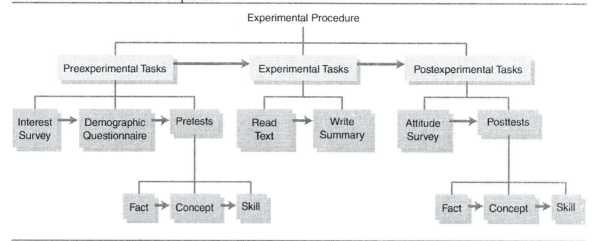

Exercise 3

Construct a sequence representation for each of the following areas.
Remember to create subsequences or subhierarchies where necessary.

1. The stages of human growth.
2. The months of the year.
3. Making pancakes.
4. Registering for classes.
5. A food chain ending with lions.
6. A course in your major area.

Matrix

A matrix organizes information in columns and rows. It's used to compare two or more things along one or more categories. Matrices show comparative relationships. Returning to the moths and butterflies matrix in Exhibit 3.3, for example, you can compare (or combine) column information, such as butterflies have two sets of wings and their wings are outstretched, and compare row information, such as moths fly at night whereas butterflies fly during the day.

Matrices are appropriate, then, whenever you're comparing two or more things. You've already seen several examples of matrices such as operant concepts (at the beginning of this chapter), whales (Exhibit 3.1), moths and butterflies (Exhibit 3.3), and schedules of reinforcement (Exhibit 3.4). Other examples might include representations comparing whole and rational numbers, types of winds,

EXHIBIT 3.16   *Hierarchy extended into a matrix.*

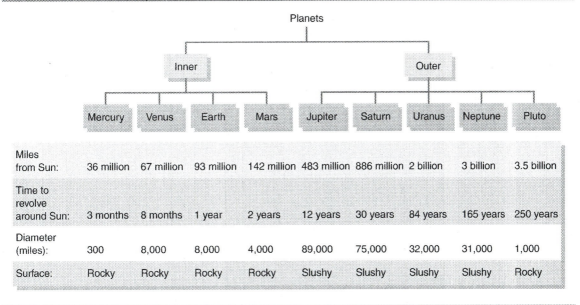

	Mercury	Venus	Earth	Mars	Jupiter	Saturn	Uranus	Neptune	Pluto
Miles from Sun:	36 million	67 million	93 million	142 million	483 million	886 million	2 billion	3 billion	3.5 billion
Time to revolve around Sun:	3 months	8 months	1 year	2 years	12 years	30 years	84 years	165 years	250 years
Diameter (miles):	300	8,000	8,000	4,000	89,000	75,000	32,000	31,000	1,000
Surface:	Rocky	Rocky	Rocky	Rocky	Slushy	Slushy	Slushy	Slushy	Rocky

historical periods, investment options, experimental findings, types of literature, U. S. presidents, and forms of representation. In fact, try to think of an instance when a comparison is not possible. Greek gods can be compared with Roman gods, igneous rock with sedimentary rock, a cumulus cloud with a stratus cloud, perimeter with area, the pancreas with the spleen, the comma with the semicolon, the Hundred Years' War with the Thirty Years' War, Pepsi with Coke, Leno with Letterman. Matrices can be used when comparing anything!

Tips for Constructing Matrices

1. Develop matrices from hierarchies and sequences. All hierarchies and sequences can be extended downward to form a matrix. For example, the planet hierarchy in Exhibit 3.9 is extended in Exhibit 3.16 to form a matrix, and the mixed fractions sequence in Exhibit 3.12 is extended in Exhibit 3.17 to form a matrix.

   These matrices were formed by adding categories to the existing hierarchy and sequence. The categories *miles from sun, time to revolve around sun, diameter,* and *surface* were added to form the planet matrix. The single category *example* was added to form the adding mixed fractions matrix. These aren't isolated examples of extending a hierarchy and sequence. Hierarchies and sequences can always be extended to form matrices.

   Suppose your chemistry instructor said that atoms are composed of protons, neutrons, and electrons. Would your instructor stop there, or would she

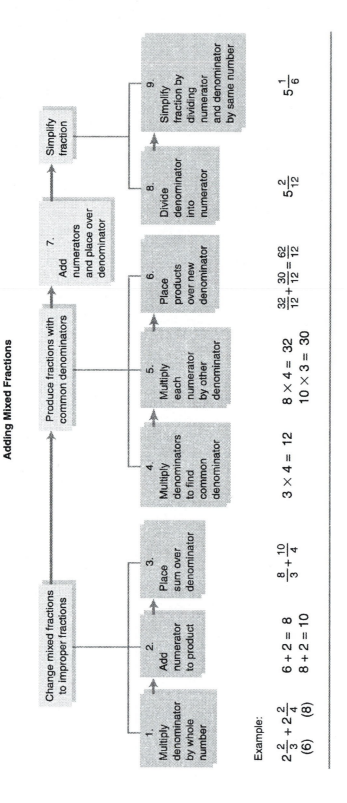

EXHIBIT 3.17   Sequence extended into a matrix.

Adding Mixed Fractions

describe several categories related to atom parts, such as *size, valence, location,* and *number?* Exhibit 3.18 shows how a hierarchy for atoms was extended into a matrix framework by adding these categories.

Or suppose your music instructor told you that there are three major periods of music: Baroque, classical, and romantic (that's a sequence). Would your instructor stop there, or would he describe several categories related to musical periods, such as *rhythm, melody, harmony,* and *composers?* You should use these categories to extend the music sequence into a matrix.

2. Construct matrices with three parts. Matrices have three parts: the *topics* that appear on top as part of a hierarchy or sequence, the *categories* that appear down the left side, and the *details* that appear in the matrix cells. Exhibit 3.19 is a matrix summarizing the matrix parts in terms of their location and description.

EXHIBIT 3.18   *Hierarchy extended into a matrix framework.*

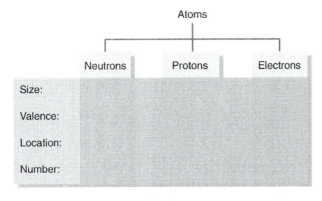

EXHIBIT 3.19   *Matrix summarizing the matrix parts.*

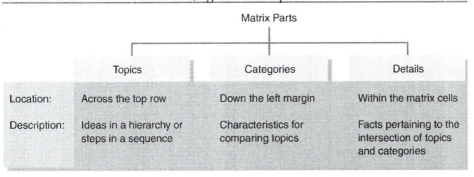

3. Be alert for certain alert words telling you that information is organized comparatively. When you hear or see these or similar words, construct a matrix:

- whereas
- however
- compare
- contrast
- different
- similar

Here are some examples:

- *Different* forms of currency:

- *Comparing* the 1970s and 1980s:

Many adjectives can potentially result in a comparative relationship and the use of a matrix. For instance, *early* settlers can be compared with *late* settlers, *domestic* flights with *international* flights, *near*sightedness with *far*sightedness, *liberal* views with *conservative* views, *zone* defenses with *man-to-man* defenses, *organic* elements with *nonorganic* elements. Be alert for adjectives and the potential comparisons they suggest.

EXHIBIT 3.20   *Matrix 1, with well-ordered topics and categories, and Matrix 2, with poorly organized topics and categories.*

Wildcats Matrix 1

	Tiger	Lion	Cheetah	Bobcat
Call:	Roar	Roar	Purr	Purr
Weight:	450	400	125	30
Life Span:	25	25	8	6
Habitat:	Jungle	Plains	Plains	Jungle
Social Behavior:	Solitary	Groups	Groups	Solitary

Wildcats Matrix 2

	Cheetah	Tiger	Bobcat	Lion
Habitat:	Plains	Jungle	Jungle	Plains
Weight:	125	450	30	400
Social Behavior:	Groups	Solitary	Solitary	Groups
Call:	Purr	Roar	Purr	Roar
Life Span:	8	25	6	25

4. Order topics and categories. My research shows that all matrices are not created equal. Some matrices make clear the relationships among details whereas others do not. It depends on the ordering of topics and categories.

For example, compare the two simple matrices in Exhibit 3.20. Although their structures are the same and they contain exactly the same information, they differ tremendously in their ability to show relationships—simply because of how their topics and categories are ordered. It is clear in Matrix 1 that cats that roar weigh more and live longer than cats that purr. Also, big and small cats can live in the jungle or plains. Jungle cats, though, live alone whereas plains cats live in groups. These relationships—so clear in Matrix 1—are all jumbled and difficult to spot in Matrix 2. Order topics and categories in ways that make relationships clear.

Exercise 4

1. Construct a matrix that compares the purposes and advantages of the parts of the SOAR study model according to what you learned in Chapter 1.

2. Construct a matrix that compares by appearance and purpose hierarchy, sequence, and matrix representations.

3. Construct a matrix that compares by location, food, atmosphere, price, and service your three favorite restaurants.

4. Construct matrix representations by extending the course-related hierarchies and sequences you developed in the exercises following the hierarchy section and the sequence section.

5. Identify the topics, categories, and details in the matrices you constructed.

Illustration

An illustration represents information pictorially. It shows what something looks like and reveals positional and sometimes dynamic (movement) relationships among its parts. Exhibit 3.21, for example, is an illustration of a braking system that shows the position of the braking parts. Exhibit 3.22 is a dynamic illustration that shows how braking parts move to slow or stop a bicycle.

Illustrations are useful across almost every subject area. In science, illustrations showing the parts of a butterfly or a bee help you learn their appearance and location. In geography, illustrations of peninsulas and isthmuses can help you learn

EXHIBIT 3.21   Positional illustration of a braking system.

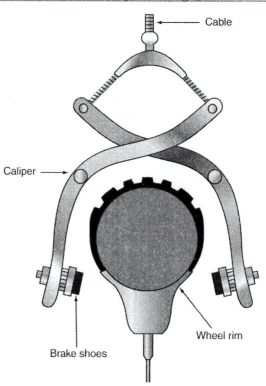

EXHIBIT 3.22   Dynamic illustration of a braking system.

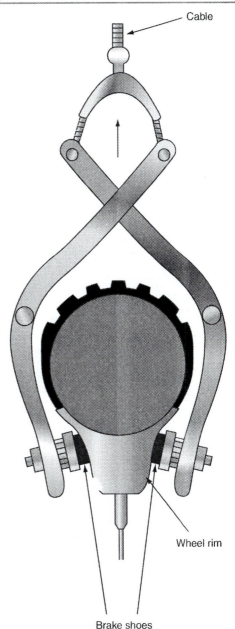

Cable

When the rider squeezes the levers (not shown), the cable forces the brake shoes to press against the wheel rim. This action slows or stops the bicycle.

Wheel rim

Brake shoes

EXHIBIT 3.23   *Illustrations included in a matrix.*

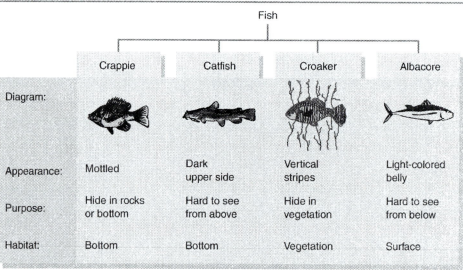

to identify these land forms. Topographical maps are illustrations that certainly depict an area's topography better than a verbal description. In mathematics, illustrations of triangles, squares, perimeters, and areas are useful for understanding these elements. And in physical education, illustrations help athletes learn positions and tactics (such as how a soccer team lines up on a corner-kick play).

Illustrations aren't necessarily alternatives to hierarchies, sequences, and matrices. They can easily be incorporated in each. A sequence that names the eight phases of the moon can be strengthened by transforming it to a matrix that includes the category *appearance* and contains illustrations of moon phases within the matrix cells.

Consider Exhibit 3.23, which shows a fish matrix. It includes an illustration of each fish within the matrix's cells. The illustrations are helpful in understanding how a fish's appearance helps it to hide from its predators or prey within its habitat.

Tips for Constructing Illustrations

1. Keep it simple. Although illustrations show what things look like, they are not exact replicas; they are representations. Include only what is necessary and don't get caught up trying to make things look realistic. Judge an illustration by its ability to show what it's intended to show. For example, the simple illustration in Exhibit 3.24 is intended to show where the four sections of the heart are relative to one another—not what the heart or sections look like exactly.

2. Use labels and captions to explain illustrations. An example is the brake part labels in Exhibit 3.21 and the caption in Exhibit 3.22. Whenever possible, place labels and captions near their referent. When text and illustrations are separated, associations between them are more difficult to make.

EXHIBIT 3.24   Illustration showing the four sections of the heart.

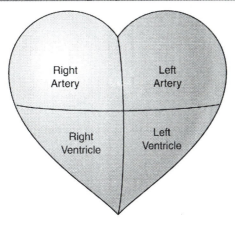

3. Be alert for certain words telling you that information can be illustrated. Words like the following might suggest an illustration representation:

- sepal, stamen, petals, anther (parts of things)
- big, hexagonal, curved, red (appearance of things)
- below, within, inside, top left (position of things)

Exercise 5

1. Construct simple illustrations of a leg and an arm that show the location of the calf, biceps, triceps, quadriceps, and hamstring muscles.
2. Construct a matrix representation that includes illustrations of geometric shapes.
3. Construct a simple dynamic illustration that shows how the earth revolves around the sun.
4. Construct an illustration for a course in your major area.

MULTIPLE REPRESENTATIONS

Sometimes a simple representation is not enough. Sometimes you need more. For instance, when studying about the human heart you might need to construct the following representations:

- an illustration showing the parts of the heart and the direction of blood flow
- a matrix comparing the major parts of the heart in terms of function, composition, and location

EXHIBIT 3.25   Multiple representations for imaginative literature.

A.

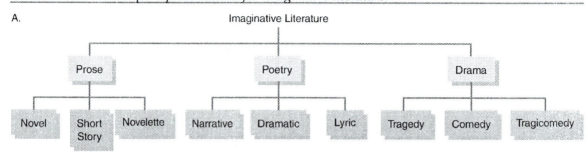

B.

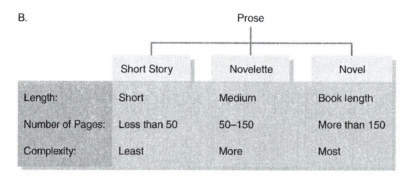

C.

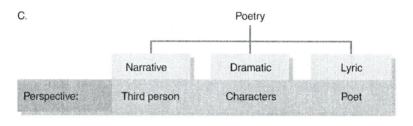

D.

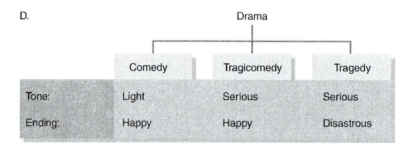

- a matrix comparing benefits and deficiencies of 0–4 chamber hearts
- a matrix comparing the transport tubes, arteries, veins, and capillaries in terms of function, location, and appearance

Exhibit 3.25 shows four representations for a unit on imaginative literatu The first hierarchy (A) overviews the three topics and their subtopics. The i maining matrix representations (B, C, and D) each develop one of the major to ics. Notice that the categories differ in representations B, C, and D. That's why th cannot be combined into a single representation. Also notice that the topics were reordered in representations B and D in order to best show the relationships among topics.

SUMMARY

Students who study effectively organize the information they select and note. They organize it in representations whenever possible to best understand and remember the relationships among the ideas. Why? It is easier to understand and remember a completed puzzle than each piece separately.

This chapter introduced you to four representations that can be used separately or in combination. Each representation is especially useful for displaying a particular type of relationship among ideas. To show once more the power of representations, the chapter's main points are summarized using the matrix representation in Exhibit 3.26.

ANSWERS TO FOCUS QUESTIONS

1. Studying a matrix produces greater learning than studying an outline because a matrix reveals relationships among ideas and an outline often obscures or hides those relationships. Here's why. A matrix makes it easy to compare two or more things because those comparisons are shown in a single matrix row. By contrast, those same things are scattered throughout an outline, making comparison difficult.

2. 1. b
   2. a
   3. c
   4. d

70

EXHIBIT 3.26 *Matrix summarizing representations.*

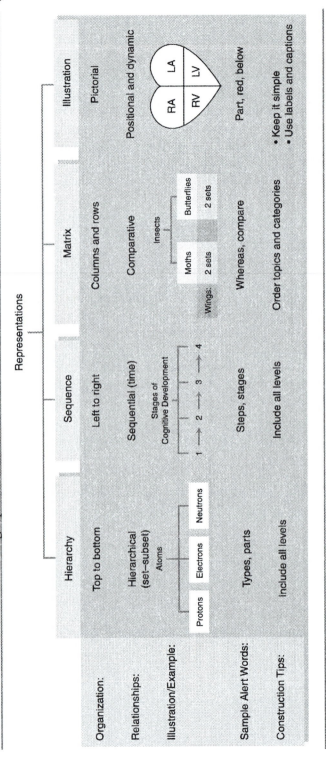

Representations

	Hierarchy	Sequence	Matrix	Illustration
Organization:	Top to bottom	Left to right	Columns and rows	Pictorial
Relationships:	Hierarchical (set–subset)	Sequential (time)	Comparative	Positional and dynamic
Illustration/Example:	Atoms — Protons, Electrons, Neutrons	Stages of Cognitive Development 1 → 2 → 3 → 4	Insects — Moths (Wings: 2 sets), Butterflies (2 sets)	Heart: RA, LA, RV, LV
Sample Alert Words:	Types, parts	Steps, stages	Whereas, compare	Part, red, below
Construction Tips:	Include all levels	Include all levels	Order topics and categories	• Keep it simple • Use labels and captions

3. 1. d
    2. c
    3. a
    4. b

4. Letters F, G, and H are the subset of C.

5. A. The alert word is *types.*

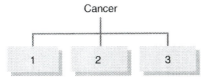

Cancer

| 1 | 2 | 3 |

   B. The alert word is *turns into.*

Embryo→Fetus

   C. The alert word is *similarities.*

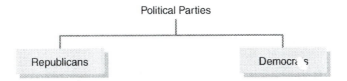

Political Parties

Republicans   Democra s

Similarity 1:

Similarity 2:

Similarity 3:

The similarities might deal with positions on foreign policy, education, and taxes.

   D. The alert word is *next to.*

Jessie   Marie

6. The representation should have multiple levels to show that there are really two main classifications of trees—conifer and deciduous.

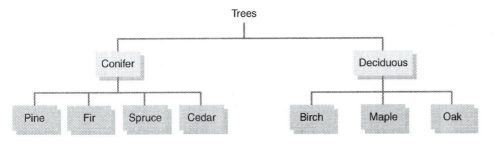

Trees

Conifer   Deciduous

Pine   Fir   Spruce   Cedar   Birch   Maple   Oak

7. Some potential categories were added to the original representations to create matrix frameworks.

   A.

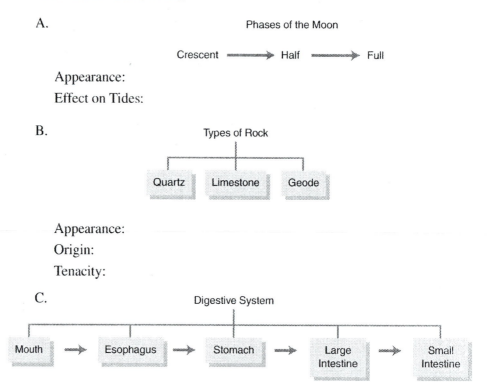

Appearance:

Effect on Tides:

   B.

Appearance:

Origin:

Tenacity:

   C.

Function:

Time:

8. The matrix should be reordered in line with the increasing value of the pieces.

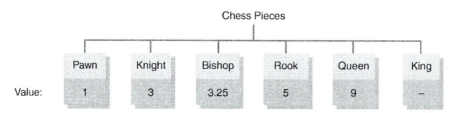

9. Three tips for constructing illustrations are (a) keep it simple, (b) use labels and captions near their referent, and (c) be alert for certain words telling you that information can be illustrated.

10. Below are some possible representations pertaining to corrective vision:

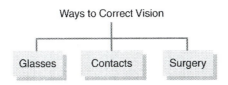

Yearly Costs:

Vision Clarity:

Comfort:

Risks:

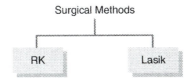

Cost:

Procedure:

Success Rate:

Healing Time:

Associate Information

4

Overview

Focus Questions

1. How effective is rehearsal for learning?

2. What proof is there that rehearsal is an ineffective learning technique?

3. What are internal and external associations?

4. You go to a family reunion. You notice how much Aunt Marge looks like cousin Paula. You learn that both Uncle Bart and Uncle Drew served in the Korean War. Uncle Marvin's stories about college remind you of your own college experiences. Which of these are internal associations and which are external associations?

5. What are two general methods for creating external associations?

6. What are first letter and keyword?

Kelly: Hey, Gabe, how did you do on that first biology quiz over cell parts and functions?

Gabe: Let's put it this way, I doubt I'll send a copy of this quiz along with my applications to medical schools. I had trouble memorizing this stuff.

Kelly: How'd you try to memorize it?

Gabe: By repeating stuff over and over. What did you do?

Kelly: I connected each cell part to a part of a city that shares the same function.

Gabe: What? Were you drinking?

Kelly: No, listen. The cell wall defines the cell's boundary and protects the cell the same way a wall might surround a city and protect it from intruders.

Gabe: I guess if they can build a wall around China you can have one around your city.

Kelly: The cell membrane allows material to be transferred in and out of the cell just like border guards and gatekeepers let people and things in and out of the city.

Gabe: The gatekeepers might allow something healthy to come in like food but not something destructive like guns.

Kelly: Exactly! The cytoplasm is the watery environment where cell functions occur. This is the city itself.

Gabe: Sounds like Venice.

Kelly: The cell nucleus is the information center. In a real city, this might be the mayor's office.

Gabe: Or the city college.

Kelly: You're catching on. The mitochondria produce energy like a . . .

Gabe: . . . power plant?

Kelly: Exactly!

Gabe: Wasn't there a plastic rectangle or something?

Kelly: You're warm—it's called the endoplasmic reticulum. These are the transport channels within the cells. I likened them to city streets.

Gabe: I can just hear you giving directions. "Go to the end of the Plasmic and make a right on Ticulum."

Kelly: Hey, that's helpful! The golgi apparatus is where secretions are packaged for discharge. What do you think I associated them with in my city?

Gabe: To our cafeteria. Just kidding! Maybe a waste treatment plant.

Kelly: You betcha.

Gabe: So that's it?

Kelly: Not quite. I also associated the cell parts to each other—showing how they relate. I made this illustration to show that the cell membrane is inside the cell wall; the nucleus and cytoplasm are inside the cell membrane; and the mitochondria, endoplasmic reticulum, and golgi apparatus are inside the cytoplasm.

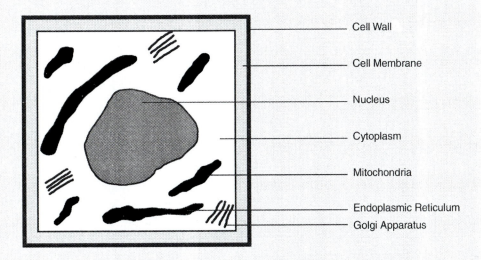

Gabe: Wow! Making associations is a lot better than trying to memorize each cell part.

Kelly: Yeah. You try that repeating stuff again and you'll be repeating biology next semester.

Kelly learned and remembered biology not because she's smart, but because she did smart things. She associated information to better understand it and remember it. As mentioned previously, students often do not-so-smart things while studying. Most often, they try to power memorize information by using rehearsal-type strategies such as repeating, recopying, and rereading. These redundant strategies are REdiculous! Doing and redoing something many times does not produce meaningful learning (even though many teachers and textbooks erroneously say that it does).

Want proof? Consider a remarkable study in which a professor who read the same 500-word prayer aloud for 25 years was suddenly tested and asked to recite

Repetition does not ensure good memory.

the prayer completely from memory. He couldn't do it. He required more than 100 promptings in order to recall it correctly.

Want more proof? Try to fill in all the numbers, letters, and symbols found on the telephone calling pad in Exhibit 4.1. You should be able to do this without "phoning a friend," considering the thousands of calls you've made and received—including the dinnertime calls from telemarketers.

Done? Okay, now check your response against the completed telephone pad in Exhibit 4.2. How did you do? Did you properly position all the numbers, letters, and symbols? Did you know that the letters begin on the second button and that the 7 and 9 buttons each contain four letters? Probably not. Most people can't remember the telephone calling pad despite the thousands of times they have used a telephone. Repeated exposure alone does not get information into your long-term memory.

Want more proof still? In class, I ask students to memorize two sets of three letters, such as BKF and VSL, by using rehearsal. Students rehearse the letters in memory for about 15 seconds and then try to recall them immediately in order. Most students recall the letters perfectly. However, when I ask them unexpectedly

EXHIBIT 4.1   *Incomplete calling pad for push-button telephone.*

EXHIBIT 4.2   Calling pad for push-button telephone.

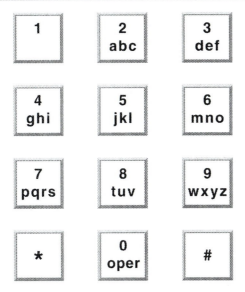

to recall the letters just a few minutes later, most cannot. Rehearsal works okay for recalling information right away, but not for recalling it later. You know this is true from your experience with telephone numbers. When you get a telephone number from directory assistance, you rehearse it before dialing it—which you do successfully. When the number is busy, however, you are, in most cases, unable to remember and redial it even a half-minute later. (Thank goodness for the redial button!) Rehearsal is effective for keeping information in memory only as long as rehearsal is occurring. When rehearsal ends, the information is soon forgotten. To retain information long term, associations must be made.

CREATING ASSOCIATIONS

It does little good to try to memorize separate pieces of information by repeating them over and over. Learning is like solving a puzzle. To learn you must connect smaller pieces until they reveal the puzzle's completed picture.

Here's an example of building connections. Suppose you had to learn the following facts about rhinos:

1. White rhinos live in grasslands.
2. White rhinos eat grass.
3. White rhinos have square lips.
4. Black rhinos have hooked lips.
5. Black rhinos eat twigs.
6. Black rhinos live in jungles.

Of course, you can try to memorize each idea separately—as most students do. Or, you can associate ideas in order to see the completed puzzle. For instance, you can associate the first and second ideas because it is logical that rhinos that live in grasslands eat grass. You can also associate the second and third ideas because square lips are well suited for scooping up and eating grass. Similarly, you can associate ideas four and five given that hooked lips are well suited for grasping and eating twigs, and you can associate ideas five and six given that twigs grow in jungles. Moreover, you can create the more general association that both black and white rhinos eat what's prevalent in their environment and have lips well suited for eating their food.

You can also associate the new information about rhinos with things you already know. For instance, you might associate the white rhino with cows, because you know that cows also live in grasslands, eat grass, and have square lips. You might also associate both types of rhinos with deer because all eat plants rather than meat.

There are two types of associations you can create when learning: internal and external. Internal associations are those made within the material being learned. You made internal associations, for example, when you related the black rhino's hooked lips to its eating of twigs, or when you related the white rhino's habitat (grasslands) to what it eats (grass). External associations are made between the new material being learned and past knowledge already stored in memory. You made an external association, for example, when you related the white rhino's habitat, lips, and food to that of the already familiar cow.

To help you remember that internal associations pertain to relationships made within the learning material and that external associations pertain to relationships made between the learning material and past knowledge, look at Exhibit 4.3, (originally presented in Chapter 1), which shows a student learning from a page of text. Remember, the *X*s represent individual text facts such as white rhinos have square lips. The broken lines represent the internal associations made among those facts. For example, the student reading about white rhinos associates facts about their habitat, food, and lips. These are internal associations because they are made within the learning material. The

EXHIBIT 4.3   *Internal and external associations.*

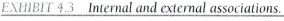
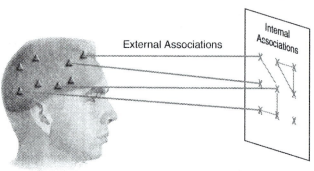

solid lines represent external associations made between the new material (the *X*s) and past knowledge stored in memory (the triangles). For example, the student might be relating white and black rhinos to deer because all three eat plants. These are external associations because the associations are made outside the learning material.

The next two sections describe internal and external associations in greater detail.

Creating Internal Associations

Creating internal associations means finding relationships among the ideas being learned. First organizing ideas into representations (as taught in Chapter 3) helps you find those relationships. Let's revisit some of the representations presented earlier and build internal associations while examining them.

Exhibit 4.4 is the schedules of reinforcement matrix first presented in Chapter 1. Examine it again now and build internal associations. A few key ones are as follows:

- Interval methods involve time; ratio methods involve number.
- Interval methods involve slow responding; ratio methods involve rapid responding.

EXHIBIT 4.4   *Matrix representation for schedules of reinforcement.*

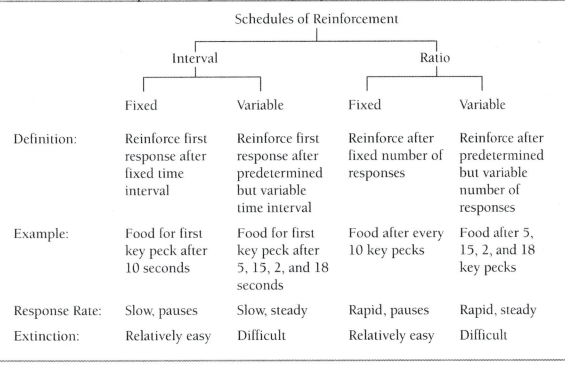

	Interval		Ratio	
	Fixed	Variable	Fixed	Variable
Definition:	Reinforce first response after fixed time interval	Reinforce first response after predetermined but variable time interval	Reinforce after fixed number of responses	Reinforce after predetermined but variable number of responses
Example:	Food for first key peck after 10 seconds	Food for first key peck after 5, 15, 2, and 18 seconds	Food after every 10 key pecks	Food after 5, 15, 2, and 18 key pecks
Response Rate:	Slow, pauses	Slow, steady	Rapid, pauses	Rapid, steady
Extinction:	Relatively easy	Difficult	Relatively easy	Difficult

- Fixed methods involve consistent reinforcement patterns; variable methods involve changing reinforcement patterns.
- Fixed methods produce pauses in responding; variable methods produce steady responding.
- Fixed methods are easy to extinguish; variable methods are difficult to extinguish.

Notice that none of these associations are available when examining each schedule-of-reinforcement fact separately. Facts must be combined in order to make internal associations and understand relationships.

Next, let's revisit the operant concepts matrix first presented in the beginning of Chapter 3 and shown here again as Exhibit 4.5. Examine it and create internal associations among the concepts before checking the following list of internal associations:

- Reinforcement involves an increase in behavior; punishment involves a decrease.
- Positive techniques involve a presented stimulus; negative techniques involve a removed stimulus.

Exhibit 4.6 is the planets matrix presented in Chapter 3. What internal associations can you create from it? Did you notice these?

- As planets increase in distance from the sun, their revolution time increases.
- Inner planets are smaller than outer planets (with the exception of Pluto).
- Inner planets have rocky surfaces whereas outer planets have slushy surfaces (with the exception of Pluto).

EXHIBIT 4.5   *Operant concepts matrix.*

		Operant Concepts	
		Behavior	
		Increase	Decrease
Stimulus	Presented	Positive Reinforcement	Positive Punishment
	Removed	Negative Reinforcement	Negative Punishment

EXHIBIT 4.6   Planets matrix.

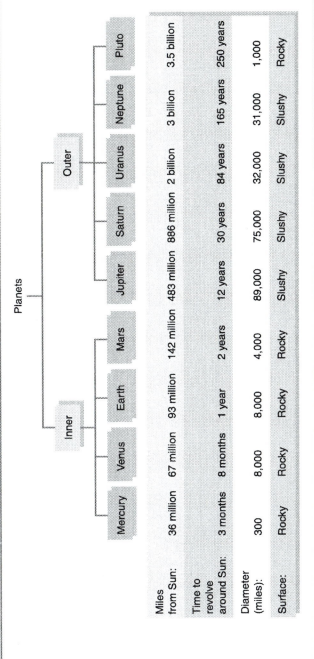

	Mercury	Venus	Earth	Mars	Jupiter	Saturn	Uranus	Neptune	Pluto
Miles from Sun:	36 million	67 million	93 million	142 million	483 million	886 million	2 billion	3 billion	3.5 billion
Time to revolve around Sun:	3 months	8 months	1 year	2 years	12 years	30 years	84 years	165 years	250 years
Diameter (miles):	300	8,000	8,000	4,000	89,000	75,000	32,000	31,000	1,000
Surface:	Rocky	Rocky	Rocky	Rocky	Slushy	Slushy	Slushy	Slushy	Rocky

EXHIBIT 4.7   *Detailed version of wildcats matrix.*

	Tiger	Lion	Jaguar	Leopard	Cheetah	Bobcat
Physical Features:						
Call:	Roar	Roar	Growl	Growl	Purr	Purr
Maximum weight (lb.):	450	400	200	150	125	30
Coat:	Yellow-orange with black stripes	Light brown	Yellow with black circles containing black spots	Yellow with black circles	Yellow with black spots	Rust color
Distinctive characteristics:	Powerful upper body	Powerful upper body	Keen eyes and ears	Tremendous strength, keen eyes and ears	Powerful, athletic legs	Keen eyes and ears
Lifestyle:						
Habitat:	Jungle	Plains	Jungle	Jungle	Plains	Jungle
Range (sq. miles):	30	150	5	15	50	30
Social behavior:	Solitary	Groups	Solitary	Solitary	Groups	Solitary
Life span (yr.):	25	25	20	10	8	6
Hunting:						
What:	Medium-size animals	Medium-size animals	Small animals	Medium-size animals	Medium-size animals	Small animals
When:	Sundown	Sunrise and sundown	Night	Night	Daytime	Night
Method:	Stalks prey Knocks prey over Hides uneaten portion for future meals	Group stalks prey from all angles Knocks prey over Will scavenge	Stalks prey Eats what it can and leaves the rest	Ambushes prey from trees Hoists prey into trees and hides for future meals	Group stalks prey Runs 65 mph to capture prey Prey often stolen by lions and hyenas Will scavenge	Ambushes prey from behind trees Eats what it can and leaves the rest
Frequency:	Weekly	Daily	Daily	Weekly	Daily	Daily

A simple wildcat matrix was presented in Chapter 3 and some internal associations were made. Exhibit 4.7 is a far more detailed wildcat matrix. Examine it carefully and the many internal associations it offers. Compare your associations with the sample ones listed here:

- Big cats roar; medium-size cats growl; small cats purr.
- The bigger the cat, the longer its lifespan.
- Jungle cats are solitary; plains cats live in groups.
- Jungle cats have smaller ranges than plains cats.
- All cats eat animals.
- Cats that eat small animals eat what they can and leave the rest.
- Cats that hunt weekly hide the uneaten portion.
- The largest cats hunt by knocking over their prey with their powerful upper bodies.
- Cats with keen eyes and ears hunt at night.
- The cheetah uses powerful legs and speed to run down prey.
- Cats that scavenge live and hunt in groups.
- Smaller cats use speed (cheetah) to hunt or ambush (leopard, bobcat) their prey.

Even a simple hierarchy, such as the punctuation hierarchy represented as Exhibit 4.8, or a simple sequence, such as the experimental procedure sequence represented as Exhibit 4.9 (both originally presented in Chapter 3), offer important internal associations. From the punctuation hierarchy, you should make these associations:

- Punctuation can come at the end of a sentence or within a sentence.
- End-of-sentence punctuation marks are a period, a question mark, and an exclamation point.
- Within-sentence punctuation marks are a comma, dash, colon, and semicolon.

EXHIBIT 4.8   *Punctuation hierarchy.*

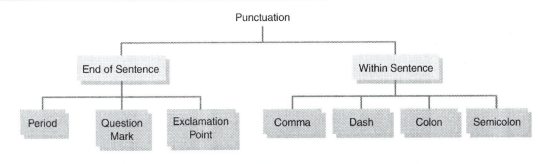

EXHIBIT 4.9   *Experimental procedure sequence.*

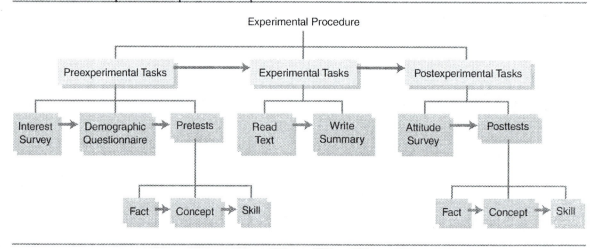

Although simple, these associations are important. I can imagine a young student aware of each punctuation mark (individual facts) but unaware which ones are used where (an internal association).

What associations can you build from the sequence in Exhibit 4.9? Compare yours with these:

- The experiment occurs in three phases: preexperimental tasks, experimental tasks, and postexperimental tasks.
- Before the experiment, participants complete an interest survey, demographic questionnaire, and pretests in that order.
- There are three pretests administered in this order: fact, concept, and skill.
- During the experiment, participants read a text and then write a summary.
- After the experiment, participants complete an attitude survey and then posttests.
- The posttests are the same as the preexperimental tasks and are administered in the same order: fact, concept, and skill.

Let's move on to some material that has not already been represented. Often-times, students believe that studying involves memorizing a list of unrelated terms. That's wrong! If those terms are part of some unit (such as schedules of reinforcement or wildcats), then they must go together in some way. Students must create associations among those terms.

Following is a list of terms to be learned from a unit on symbiosis.

- *Symbiosis.*   A situation in which two living organisms live together in a close nutritional relationship.

- *Commensalism.* A type of symbiosis in which one organism benefits and the other is unaffected.
- *Mutualism.* A type of symbiosis in which both organisms benefit.
- *Parasitism.* A type of symbiosis in which one organism benefits and the other is harmed.

Rather than try to memorize the terms one at a time, you should first construct a representation like that in Exhibit 4.10 to best organize the terms. After doing so, create internal associations among the terms, like the following:

- There are three types of symbiosis.
- All three types involve two organisms living together.
- One organism always benefits from the relationship.
- The other organism is either unaffected (commensalism), benefited (mutualism), or harmed (parasitism).

EXHIBIT 4.10 *Symbiosis matrix.*

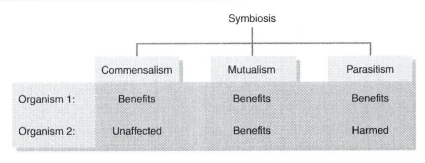

Let's look at another example of a list of terms and definitions someone might study in psychology pertaining to classical conditioning (the type of conditioning Pavlov used to get dogs to salivate in response to the sound of a bell). Hang on—the terms and definitions are, at first, going to seem as clear as an IRS tax form:

- *Classical conditioning.* The process by which a neutral stimulus that initially elicits no particular response acquires the ability to elicit the same response as another stimulus by being repeatedly paired with that stimulus.
- *Unconditioned stimulus (US).* A stimulus that can elicit a response without any prior learning or conditioning. For example, meat (US) can elicit a dog to salivate.
- *Unconditioned response (UR).* The response elicited as the result of an unconditioned stimulus. For example, showing a dog meat (US) makes it salivate (UR).

- *Neutral stimulus (NS).*   A stimulus that originally does not elicit a response. For example, ringing a bell (NS) does not make a dog salivate.
- *Conditioned stimulus (CS).*   A neutral stimulus becomes a conditioned stimulus through conditioning. The neutral stimulus is paired repeatedly with an unconditional stimulus until the neutral/conditioned stimulus alone can elicit the same response as the unconditioned stimulus. For example, repeatedly pairing a bell (NS) with meat (US) eventually makes the bell a conditioned stimulus (CS) capable of making a dog salivate.
- *Conditioned response (CR).*   The conditioned response is elicited by the conditioned stimulus and resembles the unconditioned response. For example, the dog salivates (CR) in response to the bell (CS).

Wow! Just understanding that stuff should merit a Nobel Prize. There are only six classical conditioning terms here, but it is difficult to learn them in a piecemeal fashion—one term at a time. Let's try representing this material and building internal associations.

Exhibit 4.11 is a sequence/matrix that nicely organizes the content. It shows the three simple steps of classical conditioning and an example of each step.

At a glance, the internal associations are now apparent:

- A US (meat) naturally elicits a UR (salivating).
- An NS (bell) is paired with a US (meat) several times. A UR (salivating) continues to occur because of the US (meat).
- Pairing an NS (bell) with a US (meat) transforms the NS into a CS.
- A CS (bell) elicits a CR (salivating).
- A CR (salivating) is the same as a UR (salivating).
- In summary, a dog that naturally salivates for meat learns to salivate for a bell because the bell is paired with meat.

EXHIBIT 4.11   *Classical conditioning sequence/matrix.*

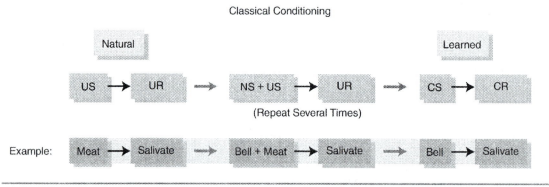

1. Below is a brief passage about the nervous system and the endocrine system. Build internal associations to help you understand their similarities and differences.

> The nervous system is composed of nerves that secrete neurohumors. Nerves also secrete noradrenaline. The nervous system helps to maintain homeostasis. Nerve responses are rapid and of short duration. Nerves transmit impulses via neurons.
>
> The endocrine system is composed of glands that secrete hormones. The adrenal gland also secretes noradrenaline. The endocrine system helps to maintain homeostasis. Endocrine responses are slow but last for a long time. Hormones are carried by the blood plasma.

2. Below is a matrix representation about fish. Build internal connections among its ideas.

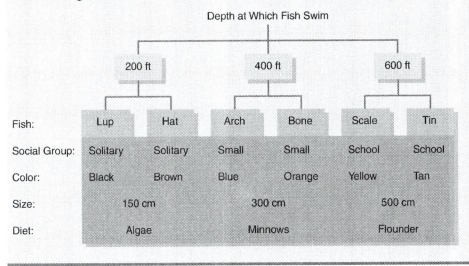

	Depth at Which Fish Swim					
	200 ft		400 ft		600 ft	
Fish:	Lup	Hat	Arch	Bone	Scale	Tin
Social Group:	Solitary	Solitary	Small	Small	School	School
Color:	Black	Brown	Blue	Orange	Yellow	Tan
Size:	150 cm		300 cm		500 cm	
Diet:	Algae		Minnows		Flounder	

Creating External Associations

Creating external associations is accomplished by relating presented material to previously acquired knowledge. When you associate new information with past knowledge, you understand the new information better and remember it more easily. Let's look at some examples of external associations.

In Chapter 1, external associations were made to learn about the four types of schedules of reinforcement. Review those now along with these new external associations:

- *Fixed ratio.* Receiving a gold star for every 100 pages read is a fixed-ratio schedule.

- *Variable ratio.* Slot machines pay off on a variable-ratio schedule.

EXHIBIT 4.12   Operant concepts matrix for creating external associations.

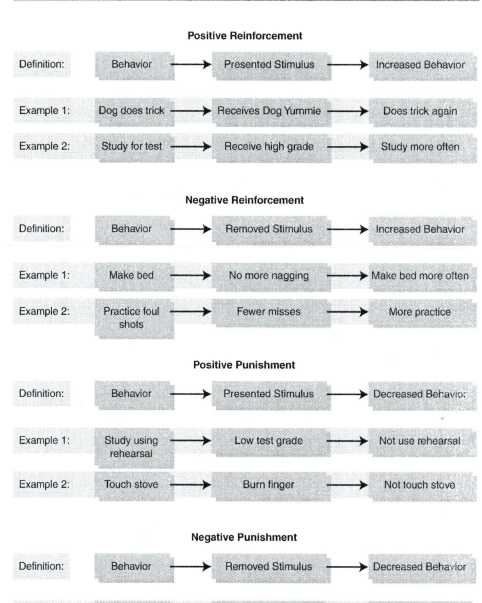

- *Fixed interval.* A weekly paycheck is received on a fixed-interval schedule.
- *Variable interval.* A car dealership that offers various discounts at various and unspecified times throughout the day to shoppers present at the dealership is using a variable-interval schedule.

Next, let's revisit and expand the operant concepts material, presented earlier in Chapter 3 and in this chapter (Exhibit 4.5), and create external associations to better understand and remember each term. Reading Exhibit 4.12 downward, you can associate the terms' definitions (the new information to be learned) with familiar examples (past knowledge). For instance, a dog doing a trick is an example of a behavior, and the dog receiving a Dog Yummie is an example of a presented stimulus. Exhibit 4.12 also shows how easy it is to include external associations in representations.

A third example of external associations comes from the material presented previously on classical conditioning (Exhibit 4.11). In Exhibit 4.13, the definition parts are associated with familiar examples. You see, for example, that a scream (US) naturally elicits fear (UR) and that pairing a neutral stimulus such as a snake with a scream eventually conditions someone to be afraid (CR) of snakes (CS). Notice how easy it is once again to add external associations to representations.

Now let's relate the symbiosis definitions presented earlier in this chapter to examples in order to make external associations. Look at Exhibit 4.14. It contains two types of examples I call near examples and far examples. Near examples are realistic examples. Crocodiles and plovers really do have a nutritional relationship that is mutualistic. Plovers eat the things lodged in crocodiles' teeth, and crocodiles get a helpful tooth cleaning. The far examples in this case are not completely accurate because they do not always involve living things (e.g., a park bench) or nutritional relationships. Still, these familiar far examples are useful for understanding and remembering whether two symbiotic parties are benefited, unaffected, or harmed. Again, these new examples are easily incorporated into representations.

EXHIBIT 4.13   *Classical conditioning matrix for creating external associations.*

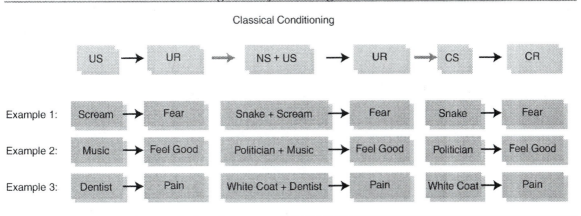

EXHIBIT 4.14   Symbiosis matrix for creating external associations.

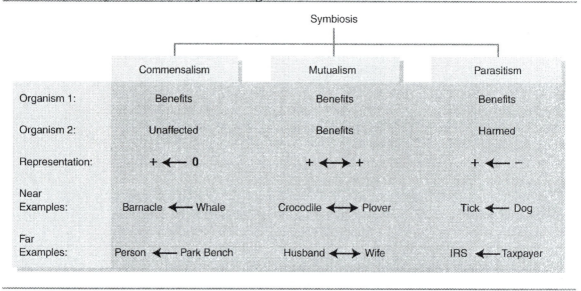

Exercise 2

1. Below is a matrix representation on figures of speech. Extend the matrix by adding new examples you create. These new examples are external associations.

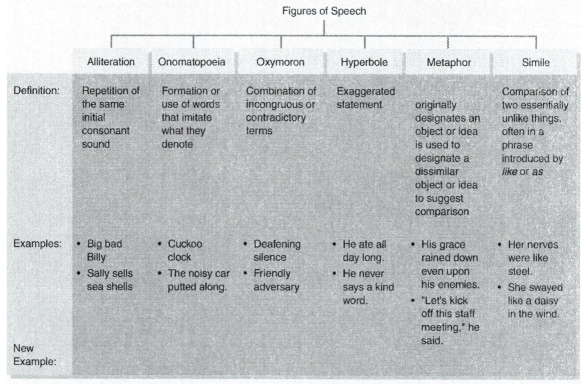

2. Generate an external association for the following definitions by relating each to a familiar example.

Reflex: an inborn, unlearned response.

■ *Example:*

Instinct: a complex, innate act performed without training.

■ *Example:*

Habit: a learned response that has become completely automatic.

■ *Example:*

We've seen that developing examples is an effective way to create external associations. Another effective technique is raising "why" questions—asking why certain things are so. Raising and answering why questions helps you to better understand and remember new information. For example, reexamine the wildcats matrix in Exhibit 4.7. Following are some why questions I raised and answered:

1. Why do bigger cats live longer? Because they are less likely to be attacked by other animals.
2. Why are lions light brown? To blend into the plains where they live.
3. Why do tigers and lions knock over their prey? Because they have powerful upper bodies.
4. Why do some cats hunt weekly? Because they hide their leftovers to eat between hunts.
5. Why do so many cats have yellowish fur? Perhaps because they live in warm climates and light colors do not get as hot.

Returning once again to the schedules-of-reinforcement material (Exhibit 4.4), I might raise and answer these why questions:

1. Why do ratio schedules produce rapid responding? Because the person can control how quickly reinforcement is given by working faster.
2. Why do fixed schedules produce pauses in responding? Because it's natural for the person to rest when reinforced and because it's predictable when the next reinforcer is available.
3. Why is it difficult to extinguish behavior reinforced on a variable schedule? Because the person never knows when reinforcement is forthcoming. It can come on the next response or a thousand responses from now; it can come in a few seconds or in a month.

Exercise 3

Below is the animal behavior passage introduced in Chapter 1. As you read it, develop external associations by attempting to generate and answer why questions.

The study of animal behavior is approached in contrasting ways by two types of psychologists: comparative psychologists and ethologists.

Comparative psychologists can be compared with ethologists along several dimensions. Comparative psychologists study animal behavior in laboratory settings. They conduct diligent experiments on a few animal species, trying to uncover general learning principles common to all animals. These American psychologists believe that behavior is learned.

Ethologists, on the other hand, study animal behavior in the animal's natural surroundings. Their methods are less rigorous. They usually observe animals. Ethologists study many animals to learn how each behaves. These European psychologists believe that behavior is innate.

We've seen so far that external associations are useful for learning packages of information such as packages relating to operant conditioning, classical conditioning, schedules of reinforcement, symbiosis, and wildcats. External associations are useful for learning more discrete or isolated facts as well.

Earlier in the chapter you were asked to remember groups of three letters. Try using external associations now to learn BKF and VSL. You could relate BKF to the phrase Burger King Fries by using each letter to begin a word in the phrase. You could relate VSL to the familiar word *visual*, which contains the consonants V, S, and L.

External associations can also be used to remember numbers such as locker combinations. As a longtime New York Yankees fan, I remembered my locker combination, 49-44-1, by connecting it to the jersey numbers worn by Yankee players. I imagined ace left-hander Ron Guidry (49) pitching to slugger Reggie Jackson (44) and volatile manager Billy Martin (1) arguing with Jackson about whether to bunt or swing away. This seems like a better way to remember combinations than movie boxing champion Rocky Balboa used in the movie *Rocky*. Even after using the same locker for about 14 years, he only remembered the combination by pulling it from a slip of paper tucked under his hat.

When you make an external association, be sure you relate the new fact to something you really know. I once made a bad connection and, as a result, learned a hard lesson. I was in college, sophomore year, when my roommate, Houser, and I visited friends at the start of school. Our friends told us their new phone number was "Columbus minus two." They explained that Columbus sailed the ocean blue in 1492; subtract two and that was their new number: 432–1490.

I was enamored by their clever memory strategy, but Houser never liked being outdone. (Later in college, Houser climbed up the side of a two-story house and onto the roof while wearing a leg cast because someone else—without a cast—had done it!) Because Houser was a history major, this phone number association challenged him all the more. Sure enough, he thought for a few minutes and then proudly reported that our new phone number was "Magellan plus five." "Simply add five to the year Magellan sailed around the world and that's our phone number," he boasted.

But the story does not end there. Late that night, in the middle of a driving rainstorm, I was downtown (probably studying) and needed a ride back to campus. I decided to call Houser and ask (beg) for a ride. (After all, what are roommates for?) Unfortunately, I had not yet learned our new telephone number and could only remember Houser's personal association, "Magellan plus five." In desperation, I pleaded for help from nearby strangers, who could only return confused expressions when asked when Magellan sailed the globe. It was a long and soggy trek back to campus. The moral of the story is that external associations won't work unless you understand your own background knowledge.

Educational psychologists have developed two especially effective memory techniques, based on building external associations, for learning and remembering facts. Each is briefly described and exemplified next.

First Letter

Transform the first letters of the information to be learned into a familiar word, phrase, or sentence. We did this earlier, transforming BKF into Burger King Fries. Here are some more examples:

- Remember the planets in order from the sun using this sentence based on the planets' first letters: "**M**y **v**ery **e**ducated **m**other **j**ust **s**erved **u**s **n**ine **p**izzas." (Mercury, Venus, Earth, Mars, Jupiter, Saturn, Uranus, Neptune, Pluto)

- Remember **HOMES** to recall the five Great Lakes (Huron, Ontario, Michigan, Erie, and Superior).

- Remember the five lines of the musical staff (E, G, B, D, F) this way: "**E**very **g**ood **b**oy **d**eserves **f**udge."

- To spell arithmetic, remember that "**a r**at **in** the **h**ouse **m**ay **e**at **t**he **i**ce **c**ream."

- Remember the order of operations in math (parentheses, exponents, multiplication, division, addition, subtraction) using the sentence, "**P**lease **e**xcuse **m**y **d**ear **A**unt **S**ally."

Keyword

The keyword method is a great technique for learning vocabulary, such as Spanish words or science terms. It's also useful for learning word pairs such as states and capitals, or authors and their works. Let's first see how it works for vocabulary. Suppose you had to learn that the Spanish word *carta* means letter. Here's what you do:

1. Create a keyword by associating *carta* with a familiar English word or phrase (the keyword) that sounds like *carta*—perhaps *cart*.

2. Create a picture or image linking the keyword (cart) to the word's meaning (letter). For example, a letter in a cart.

EXHIBIT 4.15   *The keyword method.*

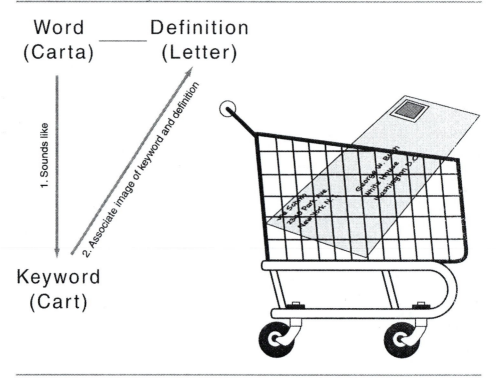

That image helps you remember that *carta* means letter. Exhibit 4.15 is a representation illustrating the keyword method.

How would you use the keyword method to learn that the Spanish word *trigo* means wheat? First, create a keyword—*trigo* sounds like tree. Second, create an image of a tree with wheat stalks growing from its trunk. This silly image helps you remember that *trigo* means wheat.

Let's try the keyword method with the science vocabulary about cell parts and functions introduced at the beginning of this chapter. The golgi apparatus has the function of packaging secretions for discharge from the cell. Create a keyword for golgi apparatus. It sounds like goalie (as in hockey) apparatus. The most obvious goalie apparatus is a mask, so imagine a goalie's hockey mask filled with sweat (a packaged secretion). To associate the term endoplasmic reticulum with its function, begin by creating a keyword. Endoplasmic reticulum sounds like plastic rectangle. To remember that the endoplasmic reticulum consists of transport channels, create an image of a rectangle made with plastic channels that marbles can move through—much like the children's toy Marbleworks. Sure, these are rather odd keywords and images, but they work. I guarantee you'll see that goalie mask filled with sweat for a long time.

EXHIBIT 4.16   The keyword method for learning states and capitals.

Now let's see how the keyword method helps you learn state capitals. Let's try Columbus, Ohio. First, create a keyword for both the capital and state. Columbus sounds like Columbus—as in Christopher Columbus. And, Ohio sounds like someone saying, "Oh, hi, you." Next, imagine Christopher Columbus greeting the Native Americans and saying, "Oh, hi, you," as shown in the upper part of Exhibit 4.16. Now, try Topeka, Kansas. Again, create a keyword for both the capital and state. Topeka sounds like toe and peek, and Kansas sounds like can. For an image associating those keywords, how about a toe peeking out of a can, like that shown in the bottom part of Exhibit 4.16?

Finally, let's use the keyword method to associate people with their literary works. For example, Thoreau wrote *Walden*. Thoreau sounds like throw. *Walden* sounds like wall. Imagine throwing something at a wall. If you want to include Thoreau's first name, Henry, imagine throwing a hen (which sounds like Henry) at a wall. (Memory techniques are not for the faint of heart.) Hawthorne wrote *The Scarlet Letter*. Hawthorne sounds like horn–thorn. Imagine a red (scarlet) letter pinned to a horn with a thorn. You can, of course, use the keyword technique to remember all kinds of pairs such as inventors–inventions, painters–paintings, teams–mascots, countries–presidents, and names–faces.

Exercise 4

1. Use the first-letter technique to learn each of the following:
   A. The progressive order of biological functioning: cells, tissues, organs, systems
   B. The order of recent presidents: Kennedy, Johnson, Nixon, Ford, Carter, Reagan, Bush, Clinton, and Bush
   C. Piaget's four stages of development: preoperational, sensorimotor, concrete, formal

2. Use the keyword method to learn the following:
   A. A fob is a short chain.
   B. A lyceum is a concert hall.
   C. A peccadillo is a minor offense.
   D. Collusion is a secret agreement.
   E. Concord is the capital of New Hampshire.
   F. Dover is the capital of Delaware.

SUMMARY

Effective studiers do not rehearse information over and over. Rehearsal strategies such as repeating, rereading, and copying are RE-diculous because they don't help you learn information long term. Effective studiers SOAR. Once you've selected (S) all the important information (through good note taking) and organized (O) it (through good representations), you should create internal and external associations (A).

Create internal associations by relating ideas within the material to be learned. Perhaps some ideas relate in a hierarchical fashion (e.g., ducks and geese are types of waterbirds), a sequential fashion (e.g., when adding mixed fractions, you first change mixed fractions to improper fractions, then find common denominators), or a comparative fashion (e.g., lions and tigers both knock down their prey while hunting). Creating internal associations is like assembling the pieces of a puzzle. Just as puzzlers assemble puzzle pieces to see the completed picture, effective studiers piece together or associate facts to understand their relationships.

Create external associations by meaningfully relating new information to past knowledge. Relating cell parts to parts of a city or relating current economic trends to those occurring in the 1980s are examples of external associations. Sometimes, meaningful associations are difficult to make. If so, use memory techniques such as first letter and keyword to associate new facts with some familiar idea—such as when we associated the cell structure golgi apparatus to a goalie's mask filled with sweat to remember that it stores secretions.

No longer be content to memorize one fact after another. Instead, associate those facts with each other and with what you already know.

ANSWERS TO FOCUS QUESTIONS

1. Rehearsal is not very effective for learning. Rehearsal holds information in memory while you rehearse it. Soon after you stop rehearsing, however, the information is forgotten.

2. There is proof that rehearsal is an ineffective strategy. A professor who rehearsed the same prayer for 25 years could not recite it from memory. You and others cannot fill in the numbers, letters, and symbols on a telephone calling pad even though you've "rehearsed" this information thousands of times. And, when given information to rehearse, such as a group of letters or a phone number, you cannot recall this information when asked for it spontaneously moments later.

3. Internal associations are relationships found among ideas being learned. External associations are relationships between the information being learned and information previously learned.

4. Internal associations are noticing the resemblance between Aunt Marge and cousin Paula and learning that Uncle Bart and Uncle Drew served in Korea. An external association is relating Uncle Marvin's college experiences to your own.

5. Two general methods for creating external associations are developing examples and raising "why" questions.

6. First letter and keyword are two memory techniques that involve using external associations to remember facts. For first letter, you use the first letter from each thing to be learned to form a meaningful word or sentence—such as using HOMES to remember the Great Lakes (Huron, Ontario, Michigan, Erie, and Superior). Keyword is used to learn vocabulary words and their meanings. You link the vocabulary word to a keyword—a familiar word it sounds like—then visually associate the keyword to the vocabulary word's meaning.

Regulate Learning

5

Focus Questions

1. What should students do prior to testing to be sure they are ready for the test?
2. Can you identify the following test items as assessing skill, concept, or fact?
   A. $847 \div 9 = ?$
   B. Who was the sixteenth president?
   C. Look at this chess diagram and circle the piece being pinned.
   D. Write the steps for solving quadratic equations.
   E. Read the examples below and underline the one that shows a monopoly.
   F. Generate a representation for the passage below.
3. What are the two main types of fact questions?
4. What is a concept?
5. Why should a concept test present novel examples to be recognized rather than ask test takers to create their own examples?
6. How do you know when you have learned a skill?
7. What are the three things you should assess when analyzing test errors?
8. What is meant by *regulate regularly*?

Billy-Bob Bo-Bennet is team manager for the North-Central Southwest Wizzahinkin Songbirds. The Songbirds defeated their arch rival, the Far-east Nearsouth Crickets, this season in Cricket Stadium. This was amazing because the Crickets are nearly unbeatable at home because their fans are the most annoying fans in all of college football. How so? Screaming fans, blaring horns, and waving hankies? Nah, that stuff's old hat. Cricket stadium is deathly quiet and then suddenly a single irritating high-pitched noise rings out from somewhere in the crowd—REEEBIT, REEEBIT, REEEBIT . . . This spine-tingling sound routinely causes the visiting team to stop playing, stand completely still, and try to locate the noise. They come together at midfield to listen. "Shhh, shhh," someone says, "I think it's coming from Section 12 in the North Stadium." "No, it's coming from Section 3 in the West Stadium," another argues. Pretty soon, there are delay-of-game penalties and players flagged for removing their helmets, as they try in vain to locate the irritating noise.

So how did team manager Billy-Bob Bo-Bennet become the team hero? He came up with some clever solutions to the Crickets's irritating fans. First, he got the coach to change the scheduled night game to a day game. The Cricket fans found it more difficult to produce this annoying chatter in a sun-lit stadium. Second, Billy-Bob suggested that the team practice in dank garages and basements throughout the summer to become accustomed to the occasional, shifting, and irritating sound of crickets. It worked. When the Songbirds arrived at Cricket Stadium, they were ready to put up with any Cricket noise. Oh, one more thing . . . Billy-Bob asked visiting Songbird fans to bring rolled up newspapers to the game.

Successful students, like successful football teams, also practice in ways that best prepare them for their big game—tests. They practice by generating and answering questions likely to appear on an upcoming test. Through this self-practice, they regulate their learning. They determine what they know and what they need to know. Successful students test themselves so thoroughly that there is no question their instructor can ask them that they haven't already asked themselves. Oh, what a confident feeling that should bring!

This chapter is about regulating learning—the **R** in SOAR. After you've selected information (S), organized it (O), and associated it (A), you need to regulate learning—determine whether you are prepared for the test. You regulate learning by generating and answering test questions of the sort likely to appear on the test. Most students, however, do not assess their knowledge prior to the test. They study by simply rehearsing information over and over. Consequently, they let instructors test them first. Only then do students find out the hard way that they don't know the material well enough. But, then it's too late.

What makes self-testing doubly unlikely is that instructors rarely tell students what kind of test questions to expect. Instead, instructors often shroud the criteria in secrecy; they simply do not reveal what type of test to expect and prepare for. This might happen because some teachers simply do not know what type of test they will give; they write it at the last minute. Or it might happen because some teachers took an oath upon becoming teachers never to tell students about tests because "no one ever told us about them when we were students." Whatever the case, students must anticipate and prepare test questions and practice answering them before the "big game."

TYPES OF TEST QUESTIONS

So what are the various types of test questions you should anticipate, prepare, and answer before an exam? Most of you have heard of multiple choice, short answer, essay, fill-in-the-blank, true/false, and the like—and believe you should expect and prepare for those. Moreover, when teachers occasionally do tell you what type of test to expect, they're likely to report that it's multiple choice or short answer or true/false. . . . Believe it or not, such information is not all that helpful. Let's see why. Look at the following questions:

1. Name the first president? (short answer)

2. The first president was _____ . (fill-in-the-blank)

3. Washington was the first president. T or F (true/false)

4. Who was the first president? (multiple choice)

   A. Alexander   C. Jefferson
   B. Hamilton   D. Washington

As you can see, there really is not much difference among these questions at all. Even though the four questions differ in form, all test exactly the same thing: knowledge of the fact that Washington was the first president. Knowing only that your test is multiple choice, or matching, or short answer tells you very little. For example, look at the following three multiple-choice questions all dealing with the area of rectangles. Would you say that these questions all test the same or different things?

1. What is the formula for finding the area of a rectangle?
   A. length + width
   B. length + length + width + width
   C. length × width
   D. length × width × height

2. Which shaded portion depicts the area of the rectangle?

A.

B.

C.

D.

3. What is the area of the rectangle below?

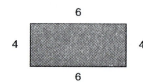

A. 10
B. 20
C. 24
D. 96

Even though all three questions are multiple choice, they clearly test different things. The first question tests *fact* knowledge: your knowledge of the fact that area equals length times width. Fact questions test whether you *know* information provided previously such as the definition of photosynthesis or the names of the U. S. presidents. The second question tests *concept* knowledge: your ability to recognize a new example of area. Concept questions test whether you can *recognize* new examples of a concept such as Renaissance art or capitalism. The third question tests *skill* knowledge: your ability to apply the area formula given a new problem. Skill questions test whether you can *apply* a skill such as adding mixed fractions or writing a computer program.

Are fact, concept, and skill knowledge—and their corresponding questions—really that different? They sure are. You might, for example, know the fact that gallbladders store bile but be unable to recognize the gallbladder (concept knowledge) given an unmarked drawing of the digestive system. Moreover, it's doubtful you could treat a diseased gallbladder (skill knowledge). Similarly, you might know the definition of a sonata (fact knowledge) but be incapable of recognizing sonatas (concept knowledge) or composing them (skill knowledge). Such is often the case when students acquire facts but fail to recognize related concepts or demonstrate related skills.

EXHIBIT 5.1   Sample fact, concept, and skill questions across subject areas.

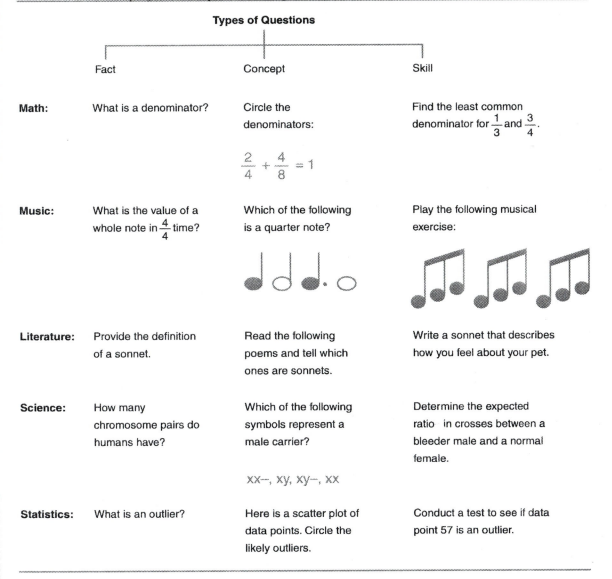

Types of Questions

	Fact	Concept	Skill
Math:	What is a denominator?	Circle the denominators: $$\frac{2}{4} + \frac{4}{8} = 1$$	Find the least common denominator for $\frac{1}{3}$ and $\frac{3}{4}$.
Music:	What is the value of a whole note in $\frac{4}{4}$ time?	Which of the following is a quarter note?	Play the following musical exercise:
Literature:	Provide the definition of a sonnet.	Read the following poems and tell which ones are sonnets.	Write a sonnet that describes how you feel about your pet.
Science:	How many chromosome pairs do humans have?	Which of the following symbols represent a male carrier? xx--, xy, xy--, xx	Determine the expected ratio in crosses between a bleeder male and a normal female.
Statistics:	What is an outlier?	Here is a scatter plot of data points. Circle the likely outliers.	Conduct a test to see if data point 57 is an outlier.

So, what type of test questions should you expect and practice for—fact, concept, or skill? Probably all three. Exhibit 5.1 shows how fact, concept, and skill questions are all possible in various subjects. The questions illustrated should look familiar to you. Your teachers have always assessed your ability to recall facts, recognize examples, and apply skills. Let's look more closely now at the three types of questions and how you should regulate learning for each type.

Exercise 1

Identify the following test items as being fact, concept, or skill items.

Insert quotation marks if appropriate in items 1 and 2.

1. Making fun of Cooper, Mark Twain said, He saw nearly all things as through a glass eye, darkly.

2. Mark Twain said that Cooper saw nearly everything darkly, as if he were looking through a glass eye.

3. Name the three instances when quotation marks are necessary.

4. When are double quotation marks used?

5. Should the following sentence contain quotation marks? The poem Twas the Night Before Christmas is a holiday favorite.

Regulate Fact Learning

Most test questions are fact questions that test your memory for previously presented information. Fact items are likely to turn up in all courses, from art to zoology. They are most prevalent in information courses such as history, psychology, sociology, and philosophy. They are less prevalent in skill courses such as math or chemistry. Regulate fact learning by generating and answering fact questions in advance of the test.

There are two main types of fact questions: single fact and relational fact. *Single-fact questions* require you to know a single fact such as black rhinos are solitary. *Relational-fact questions* require you to know related facts such as white rhinos are bigger than black rhinos.

If you adequately select and organize information (the *SO* in SOAR), by creating complete and organized notes, then generating fact questions is a snap. Let's revisit the planets matrix shown here as Exhibit 5.2. From it you can easily generate single-fact questions by asking for details associated with a topic and category. For instance, you can generate a question about Earth's (topic) diameter (category) such as: What is Earth's diameter? Or you could generate a question about Jupiter's (topic) surface (category) such as: Is Jupiter's surface slushy or rocky? Some other possible single-fact questions include the following:

- What is Pluto's revolution time?
- What is the diameter of Mars?
- How many miles is Neptune from the sun?

The matrix is equally helpful in generating relational-fact questions. Generate these by comparing information across a single category such as "miles from sun" (e.g., Which planet is farthest from the sun?) or across multiple categories such as "miles from sun" and "time to revolve around sun" (e.g., As planets increase in miles from the sun, it takes _____ time to revolve around the sun.)

EXHIBIT 5.2   *Planets matrix.*

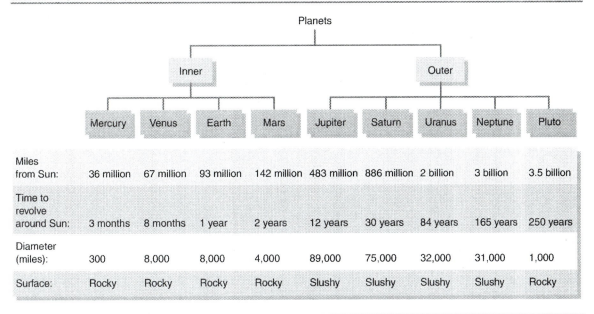

	Mercury	Venus	Earth	Mars	Jupiter	Saturn	Uranus	Neptune	Pluto
Miles from Sun:	36 million	67 million	93 million	142 million	483 million	886 million	2 billion	3 billion	3.5 billion
Time to revolve around Sun:	3 months	8 months	1 year	2 years	12 years	30 years	84 years	165 years	250 years
Diameter (miles):	300	8,000	8,000	4,000	89,000	75,000	32,000	31,000	1,000
Surface:	Rocky	Rocky	Rocky	Rocky	Slushy	Slushy	Slushy	Slushy	Rocky

Other sample relational-fact questions are as follows:

- Which planet has the smallest diameter?
- Which planets have rocky surfaces?
- Generally speaking, are inner planets smaller or larger than outer planets?
- What is the relationship between diameter and surface?

Now practice generating fact questions from the wildcats matrix re-presented here as Exhibit 5.3. Here are some sample questions:

Single Fact

- What call does the tiger make?
- Where does the lion live?
- Does the bobcat live alone or in groups?
- How much does the cheetah weigh?

Relational Fact

- Which cats live in groups?
- Which cats purr?
- What's the relationship between weight and life span?
- Do jungle cats live alone or in groups?

EXHIBIT 5.3   *Wildcats matrix.*

Wildcats				
	Tiger	**Lion**	**Cheetah**	**Bobcat**
Call:	Roar	Roar	Purr	Purr
Weight:	450	400	125	30
Life Span:	25	25	8	6
Habitat:	Jungle	Plains	Plains	Jungle
Social Behavior:	Solitary	Groups	Groups	Solitary

Using the matrix as a guide, you can easily generate every single-fact and relational-fact question that might possibly appear on a test.

Exercise 2

Below is a matrix representation for types of measurement. Generate single-fact and relational-fact questions for this material.

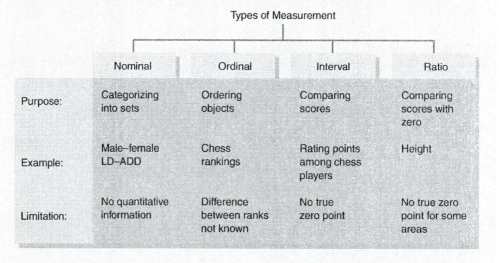

	Nominal	**Ordinal**	**Interval**	**Ratio**
Purpose:	Categorizing into sets	Ordering objects	Comparing scores	Comparing scores with zero
Example:	Male–female LD–ADD	Chess rankings	Rating points among chess players	Height
Limitation:	No quantitative information	Difference between ranks not known	No true zero point	No true zero point for some areas

Regulate Concept Learning

Concepts are things that are defined and have examples. *Square* is a concept. Its definition is "a closed, four-sided figure, with all sides equal." There are countless examples of squares—large ones, small ones, dark ones, light ones. . . . The concept of square is easily tested by presenting students with several geometric figures including rectangles, triangles, circles, and squares and asking them to mark all the squares. If they do so correctly, they've acquired the concept of square.

The world is filled with concepts. Look around you; you've learned to recognize *books, lamps, pencils, sweaters, shoes, walls, carpets, windows, trees, cars, clouds* . . . all concepts. Your concept knowledge is even more exact. You can probably recognize various types of sweaters, such as *V-neck, turtleneck,* and *cardigan,* and various types of clouds, such as *cumulus, stratus,* and *cirrus.* You can even recognize more abstract concepts when you experience them, such as *love, justice,* and *courage.*

School learning abounds with concept learning. Biology students might need to recognize new examples of *absorption, mixtures, compounds, sea urchins, commensalism,* and *mitochondria.* Psychology courses are laden with concepts such as *punishment, reinforcement, fixed-ratio schedules, retroactive interference, unconditioned stimuli,* and *independent* and *dependent variables.* In architecture classes, students must recognize new examples of various architectural structures such as *gothic, colonial,* and *tudor.* In music classes, students recognize musical compositions by period (such as *classical* and *romantic*) and by composer (such as *Bach, Haydn,* and *Stravinsky*). In art classes, artistic styles are identified (such as *cubism* and *impressionism*), as are more obscure works of well-known artists (such as *van Gogh* and *Rembrandt*). In literature, a student might have to classify the form of poetry (*narrative, dramatic,* or *lyric*) or recognize the style of *Emily Dickinson* or *Walt Whitman.* Mathematics, too, is rich with concepts. Geometric shapes such as *circle, square, ellipse,* and *parallelogram* must be recognized. Math students must also recognize types of problems so they know what formula to apply. For example, a student must recognize this as a *subtraction problem:* "John had 14 marbles and gave 7 to Bill. How many marbles did John have left?" If the student misclassifies the problem as an *addition problem,* the student gets the wrong answer even though he or she knows how to add and subtract. Oftentimes, students who have good math skills get the wrong answer anyway because they misclassify math problems. They fail to recognize math concepts.

You should regulate concept learning by generating and answering concept questions in advance of the test. Good concept questions require that students recognize new examples of the concept. So, when practicing for concept questions follow these guidelines:

1. Do Not Test Facts

The following are fact questions because they require knowledge of previously provided facts or related facts:

- What is the definition of positive reinforcement?
- Which two operant techniques involve a decrease in behavior?

The following is a concept item because it requires the recognition of an example:

- Sam wore green socks and scored 100 percent on his math test. He wore the same socks for the next math test. Sam's superstitious behavior is best explained by _____ .

  A. positive punishment

  B. positive reinforcement

  C. negative punishment

  D. negative reinforcement

Be cautious that you don't develop fact questions disguised as concept questions. The following item seems to present an example to be recognized. But, when you look more closely, you see that the example is really nothing more than a restatement of the concept's definition.

- When Billy did good things, the teacher presented a stimulus to increase those behaviors. This is an example of _____ .

A much better item follows:

- When Billy looked attentive, the teacher nodded approvingly at Billy. After a while, Billy paid attention with greater regularity. This is an example of _____.

2. Do Not Ask for Examples

When constructing concept items, require test takers to *recognize* provided examples rather than have them provide examples. Here's why. Suppose I tell you during instruction that "jumbo shrimp" is an example of an oxymoron. On the test I ask for an example of an oxymoron and you say "jumbo shrimp." If this occurred, you would be correct but simply repeating a fact that I had previously told you. There is no evidence that you could actually recognize a new example. Even if I told you to provide an example not provided in class, the same problem arises. Perhaps a friend told you that "deafening silence" is an oxymoron and you provide that example as your test answer. Again, you are simply repeating a fact. Just because you know the fact that "deafening silence" is an oxymoron does not mean you can recognize new examples. To drive this important point home, consider a very young child who can state that her neighbor Mrs. Kravitz is a busybody because that's how her parents refer to Mrs. Kravitz. Although the child can easily name Mrs. Kravitz as an example of a busybody (and just might do so when she sees her), it's unlikely she could herself recognize other examples of the concept.

3. Do Not Include Familiar Examples

It is important that test takers recognize new, previously unencountered examples to prove they've learned concepts. Therefore, do not repeat examples used in class. And, do not use examples similar to those used in class.

For example, while teaching the concept of positive reinforcement, the teacher uses this example: "Each time the dog rolled over, the dog trainer gave him a Dog Yummie and the dog quickly learned the trick." When generating practice questions, do not use this familiar example or alter it meaninglessly by changing the behavior from rolling over to lying down, replacing the dog trainer with a child, or substituting a cracker for a Dog Yummie. These cosmetic changes make it too easy to identify the "new" example as one previously encountered.

4. Test Concepts Amid Related Concepts

A concept is rarely learned in isolation. When learning about the geometric concept square, it's likely you'll learn about related concepts such as triangle, rectangle, and rhombus. Positive reinforcement is learned with related concepts such as negative reinforcement, positive punishment, and negative punishment. Unconditioned stimuli are learned along with conditioned stimuli, neutral stimuli, unconditioned responses, and conditioned responses. Oxymoron is learned among other figures of speech such as alliteration, onomatopoeia, and hyperbole.

When testing concept knowledge—the ability to recognize new examples—it's best to have people recognize concepts against a backdrop of related and potentially confusing concepts. This is not only the strongest test for concept knowledge; it is the most realistic. In the real world, cumulus clouds must be discriminated from cirrus clouds, elm trees from birch trees, and stop signs from yield signs.

Therefore, test concepts by having test takers discriminate them from closely related concepts. Here are two good examples:

1. A remora fish uses a sucker on its dorsal fin to attach itself to a shark. When the shark feeds, the remora picks up floating scraps. The shark is not inconvenienced. This is an example of _____ .
   A. parasitism
   B. commensalism
   C. mutualism

A concept is rarely learned in isolation— instead, it's likely you'll learn about related concepts.

2. Small fish live among the tentacles of a sea anemone's stinging cells. They derive protection and some food. What kind of relationship is this?
   A. predation
   B. scavenging
   C. symbiosis

The first item forces test takers to discriminate the example of commensalism from two other related forms of symbiosis: mutualism and parasitism. The second item forces test takers to recognize symbiosis from two related types of food relationships: predation and scavenging.

5.   Share Practice Tests with Study Partners

Developing concept test items is a great way to practice for concept tests, but you should do more. You should share practice tests with study partners. Here's why. Remember that concept tests require you to *recognize* new examples, not generate new examples—which is exactly what you are doing when you construct concept tests. Therefore, it is helpful to exchange practice tests with study partners so that group members also get practice doing what they must ultimately do on the test—recognize new examples. The more practice you get recognizing novel examples, the better prepared you'll be for concept test items. In Chapter 6, other advantages of group study are described.

Exercise 3

Using the same representation for types of measurement used in the previous exercise, generate several concept questions following the guidelines presented in this section.

Regulate Skill Learning

What is the solution to this problem: $3 + 6 \times 4 =$ _____ ? Is it 36 or 27? Do you first add 3 and 6 and then multiply the sum by 4 (to get 36), or do you first multiply 6 and 4 and then add 3 to that product (to get 27)? The correct answer is 27; you must multiply 6 and 4 first. Why? Because there is a *rule* that governs how to solve this problem and all problems containing assorted arithmetic operations. The order-of-operations rule states that you always conduct operations in this order: parentheses, exponents, multiplication, division, addition, and subtraction. That's why it was correct to multiply before adding in this problem. Rules are one form of skill knowledge. The application of rules is one type of skill for which you should regulate learning.

What is the solution to this problem: The five members of the study group had scores of 90, 95, 95, 100, and 98 on the history test. What was the group's average? The solution is 95.6. Finding the correct solution involves applying a *procedure*.

The procedure for calculating the mean is (1) sum all the scores and (2) divide the sum by the number of scores. Procedures, then, are a second form of skill knowledge. The application of procedures is a second type of skill for which you should regulate learning.

To summarize, skill questions ask that you apply rules or procedures you've learned. Don't confuse skill questions with fact questions. One's to know and one's to show. Fact questions require you to know information; skill questions require you to show how it is applied. For instance, stating the order of operations is stating a fact. Applying the order of operations to solve a math problem is a skill. Stating the formula for calculating the mean is a fact. Applying the formula to calculate the mean is a skill.

Let's look at some other examples of rules and procedures you probably already learned in school.

Rules

Should you ask, "John went to the store with who?" or "John went to the store with whom?" "Whom" is correct according to the rule, "use whom in the objective case." The objective case occurs when a word is an object of a preposition such as *with, for, to,* and *in.* Should you say, "To who will you send it?" or "To whom will you send it?" The same rule governs your answer: use whom because it is the object of the preposition *to.* If you apply this rule correctly, you should never make a faux pas regardless whom you speak to.

How do you solve this math problem: $7 - -10 = $ ___ ? The solution is 17. This problem, and all others involving the subtraction of a negative number, is easy to solve if you apply the rule, "If you are subtracting a negative number, then switch the negatives to positives so that you are adding a positive number instead." Once you acquire this rule, you can easily solve this and similar problems too: $-13 - -14 = $ ___ .

You've learned several spelling rules such as "i before e except after c," and "drop the e and add ing." The first helps you spell tricky words such as *receipt* and *receive.* The second helps you convert words such as *love* to *loving* and *joke* to *joking.*

Rules also help in pronunciation. The *o* in cone is long because the word ends in *e.* The *i* in mine is long for the same reason. The rule is that one-syllable words following the form "consonant–vowel–consonant–e" have long vowel sounds and a silent ending *e.*

Stating a rule is not the same
as applying it.

You've also learned several studying rules such as the following:

■ If the material is comparative, then generate a matrix.

■ If it is difficult to record complete notes, then tape-record the lecture.

■ If you must miss class, then arrange for a classmate to tape it.

■ If you encounter alert words such as *parts, types, characteristics,* and *kinds,* then construct a hierarchy.

■ If relationships are not clearly presented in a matrix, then try reordering topics and categories.

Note that all rules can be expressed as if/then statements. If a certain condition exists (e.g., a math problem containing parentheses), then you should take a certain course of action (e.g., do the operation contained in the parentheses first). Identifying the *if* portion of the rule (e.g., the parentheses) is recognizing a concept. Thus, you can see that concept recognition is an important part of applying rules.

Procedures

Some skills are more complex than applying single rules. They require that you combine rules and concepts in a procedural (step-by-step) way. Consider this problem:

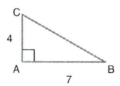

What is the length of line CB?

The procedure used to solve this problem involves the following steps comprising concepts and rules:

1. Recognize the figure as a right triangle (concept).
2. Recognize the hypotenuse (line BC) (concept).
3. Recognize the length of the given sides (4 and 7) (concept).
4. Square the given sides ($4^2 = 16$, $7^2 = 49$) (rule).
5. Sum the squares ($16 + 49 = 65$) (rule).
6. Find the square root of the summed squares by division ($\sqrt{65} = 8.06$) (rule).

This procedure, known as the Pythagorean Theorem, is applicable for any problem aimed at determining the length of a right traingle's unknown side.

Procedures are naturally represented as sequences, as explained in Chapter 3. You can revisit those plus examine Exhibit 5.4, which shows the procedure for cal-

EXHIBIT 5.4   Procedure for calculating the hypotenuse of a triangle.

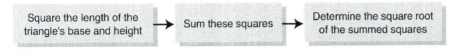

EXHIBIT 5.5   Procedure for calculating a standard deviation.

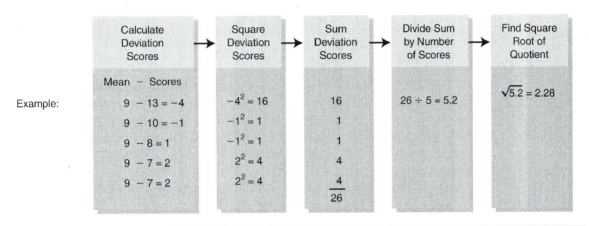

culating the hypotenuse of a triangle, and Exhibit 5.5, which shows the procedure for calculating a standard deviation.

What other procedures do you know or might need to learn? In math, you apply procedures for solving quadratic equations, doing long division, and calculating percentiles. In science, you use procedures when you balance chemical equations, compute genetic makeup, and calculate force. In English, you compose correctly punctuated sentences and well-structured essays. When studying you construct representations, create internal associations, and employ the SOAR study model.

Practice Tips

Practice is crucial for acquiring skills. As you practice motor skills such as playing baseball or intellectual skills such as adding mixed fractions, your performance becomes more accurate and more automatic. Through practice you can throw and catch a ball without even thinking about it. The same is true for changing a fraction such as $1\frac{3}{8}$ to $\frac{11}{8}$. Because you've practiced similar fraction problems, you can solve this one with minimal thought and effort.

As was true for fact and concept learning, you should regulate skill learning by generating and answering skill items before an exam. Here are some skill-practice tips:

1.   Be Sure the Items You Write Are Really Skill Items

Asking "What is the procedure for adding mixed fractions?" is a fact item. A parrot could learn to simply state that fact. Asking "Which of the following fractions is a mixed fraction?" is a concept item. The student need only recognize an example of a mixed fraction. Asking "What is the sum of $3\frac{3}{4} + 2\frac{1}{7}$?" is a skill item because it requires students to apply a skill.

2.   Provide New Problems

If your instructor told you that the hypotenuse of a triangle with a base of 4 and height of 3 was 5, then it's possible you might recall that solution from memory when later given the same problem. If so, you are recalling a fact, not applying a skill. Be sure to generate new skill items that do not repeat problems introduced during instruction. A novel Pythagorean Theorem problem is easy to generate, such as "What is the hypotenuse of a right triangle with a base of 7 and height of 6?"

Because skill questions on a test can come in many forms, be sure to vary the form of your practice problems. Here are a variety of problems dealing with the Pythagorean Theorem:

- What is the hypotenuse of a triangle with a base of 9 and height of 7?
- What is the length of side AB?

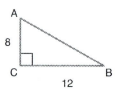

- What is the length of side XY?

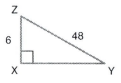

■ Use the picture below to answer the following question.

Bill's House

Tina's House

Cindy's House

The distance from Bill's house to Tina's is 2 miles. Bill's house to Cindy's is also 2 miles. Assuming Bill's house forms a right angle between Cindy's and Tina's houses, what is the distance between Cindy's and Tina's houses?

3. Share Practice Tests with Study Partners

To best acquire skills, you need a lot of practice with a variety of problems. An effective way to accomplish this is to share your practice items with study partners. That way, you enjoy the benefits of generating new skill questions and answering them. Moreover, your study partners can offer valuable feedback before the instructor does. For instance, you might be incorrectly applying the Pythagorean Theorem or incorrectly adding mixed fractions. It's best to have study partners check your skill level and offer pointers before your instructor does.

Exercise 4

1. Generate two skill items in the area of adding mixed fractions.
2. Generate two skill items pertaining to using commas appropriately.
3. Generate two skill items related to SOAR.

AFTER THE TEST IS OVER

Contrary to popular belief, the learning process does not end when the test is over. You should regulate your learning then, too. There is still much to learn. Consider football. When the game is over, coaches and players spend hours breaking down film of the game, looking for mistakes players made so they can be corrected before the next game. Or, consider chess. Chess players notate their games in order to analyze them afterward with a computer or chess coach. This analysis uncovers weak moves that can be improved in future games. You too should analyze test errors in order to improve study behaviors and your performance on future tests.

When a graded test is returned to you, don't just look at the score and put the test away. Analyze your errors to see what went wrong. Specifically, analyze the error content, type, and source. The *content* pertains to the topic of the test question. Perhaps the question covered the topic of negative reinforcement or classical conditioning. The *type* of question pertains to whether the item assessed fact, concept, or skill knowledge. The test item "Define positive reinforcement" is, for example, a fact item. The error *source* refers to why the error occurred. According to the SOAR model, a test error might occur because of the failure to select and note key ideas, to organize ideas, to create internal and external associations, or to regulate learning.

Let's look at an example. Following is a graded 10-item test on the measurement topic central tendency. Suppose you answered five questions correctly and earned a score of 50 percent. Don't be satisfied just knowing your score—especially that one! Analyze your errors and determine what went wrong and why.

Test on Central Tendency

    1. What score occurs most?

✗   2. What score divides a set of scores?

    3. What is the sum of all scores divided by the number of scores?

    4. What measure of central tendency is affected by extreme scores?

    5. To find out how students did on the test, Mr. Marsh added all the scores and divided by the number of total scores. What did Mr. Marsh find?

✗   6. There are 25 students in Ms. Brom's class. She arranged their test scores from highest to lowest. The thirteenth score on the test represented what?

✗   7. Looking over the height chart for her volleyball team, the coach said, "It looks like most of you are 5 feet 8 inches." What concept has the coach expressed?

For items 8 through 10, use the following scores: 5, 2, 4, 5, 6, 8, 5

✗   8. Calculate the mean.

✗   9. Calculate the median.

   10. Calculate the mode.

You can set up your analysis in a matrix as shown in Exhibit 5.6. From this analysis, it's easy to see *what* went wrong. In terms of *error type*, you missed

EXHIBIT 5.6   *Error analysis showing item type and content, with X indicating items missed.*

Item Number	Type	Content
1	Fact	Mode
✗ 2	Fact	Median
3	Fact	Mean
4	Fact	Mean
5	Concept	Mean
✗ 6	Concept	Median
✗ 7	Concept	Mode
✗ 8	Skill	Mean
✗ 9	Skill	Median
10	Skill	Mode

mostly concept items (numbers 6 and 7) and skill items (numbers 8 and 9). You only missed one fact item (number 2). In terms of *error content,* most errors pertained to the median (numbers 2, 6, and 9). One item each was missed pertaining to the mode (number 7) and mean (number 8).

Now that you know what went wrong in terms of content and type, next look at *why* these errors occurred. Determine their source.

You missed three items (numbers 2, 6, and 9) pertaining to the median. You check your lecture notes on central tendency and note that there are no notes about median. You missed class that day because of a dental appointment and did nothing to gather complete notes later. The error source, then, is not selecting and noting key ideas for further study (the *S* in SOAR).

Item 7 is a concept item about mode. You misclassified this example as the mean. You look back in your study notes and realize that you did not make internal associations comparing examples of the three types of central tendency. Furthermore, you note that your practice concept questions are really fact questions. You therefore chalk this missed item up to not making associations (the *A* in SOAR) and to inadequate regulation of your learning (the *R* in SOAR).

Finally, you note that you missed two skill items. A quick check of your study notes reveals that you never practiced generating and answering skill questions (again, the *R* in SOAR). This omission explains your weak skill performance.

Knowing what errors you made; why you made them; and, of course, how to use SOAR should guarantee improved performance on retests and all future tests.

Exercise 5

Below is a 10-item test on grammar. Suppose you had answered the items marked with Xs incorrectly. Conduct an error analysis to learn what you got wrong. Provide some possible reasons for why you missed those items. (The information in parentheses did not appear on the test but is presented to help in your analysis.)

1. Define a restrictive clause.

2. What is the difference between a restrictive clause and a nonrestrictive clause?

Underline the restrictive clauses in the items below:

✗　　3. The two things most universally desired are power and admiration.—Bertrand Russell.

✗　　4. He spent long hours caring for the children who were sick with the AIDS virus.

Underline the nonrestrictive clauses in the items below:

5. This intrigued Newton, who sought knowledge in many strange places.—Joseph F. Goodavage

6. He unbuttoned his coat with its shiny silver buttons like a child.

✗　　7. An experienced public speaker does not fear public speaking generally speaking. (nonrestrictive)

✗　　8. An experienced public speaker generally speaking does not fear public speaking. (nonrestrictive)

✗　　9. Students who use drugs tend to earn lower grades. (nonrestrictive)

✗　　10. Aunt Maple my Dad's sister is coming for dinner Thursday evening. (nonrestrictive)

REGULATE REGULARLY

You've seen that in order to SOAR to success you need to regulate learning by self-testing before exams and by analyzing errors afterward. Actually, there's more to regulation. Successful students regulate their learning at all times. They regulate regularly. Look at all the things you can regulate. When learning from lectures regulate whether you're prepared emotionally, physically, and mentally to learn; whether you are noting all the main ideas, details, and examples; and whether you are revising notes effectively following the lecture. Regulate how well you are organizing lecture ideas and creating associations—internal and external. Also, regulate your self-testing. Do the questions you pose adequately cover the content and possible question types? Can you adequately answer these questions and those provided by study group members? The next chapter discusses other aspects of studying such as where and when to study. You should regulate those things. And, what about motivation, the topic of Chapter 7? You should, of course, regulate your motivation.

Successful learners regulate all aspects of learning. They talk with the "little teacher inside their brain," who is continually asking questions of them, such as "Are you using your time wisely?" and "What external associations can be made here?" When that little teacher inside your brain starts talking to you, don't seek an exorcism or call Ghostbusters. Accept and relish your self-regulation, because if you don't regulate your own learning, then you'll probably find out the hard way that you don't know all that you need to know.

SUMMARY

This chapter addressed how to regulate learning (the *R* in SOAR) by preparing for three types of test questions: fact, concept, and skill. Fact questions tap your knowledge of previously presented information—either single facts or related facts. Concept questions assess your ability to recognize new examples. Skill questions determine whether you can apply a skill in a new setting. Instructors include these types of questions on tests, so you should regulate learning by generating and answering these types of questions in advance of the test. It is also important to share your practice items with study partners. This widens and strengthens your self-regulation. Also, you should analyze your test errors following tests to improve future study and test performance. Analyze errors in terms of content, type, and source. Finally, regulate learning regularly—while learning from lectures and texts, constructing representations, creating associations, arranging a study routine, and controlling motivation.

ANSWERS TO FOCUS QUESTIONS

1. Students should know whether or not they are ready for a test by testing themselves so thoroughly that there is nothing the instructor can later ask them that they have not already asked themselves.

2. A. Skill
   B. Fact
   C. Concept
   D. Fact
   E. Concept
   F. Skill

3. The two main types of fact questions are single fact and relational fact.

4. Concepts are things that can be defined and have examples. Triangles are concepts. The definition of a triangle is "a closed three-sided figure." Below is an example:

5. Instructors know students have learned a concept when students can recognize new examples of the concept. For instance, instructors know students have acquired the concept of alliteration when they can recognize a new example of it. Providing its definition would reveal only fact learning. For a student to create his or her own example may not be sufficient because it might be an example the student learned previously. To demonstrate concept learning, new examples must be identified.

6. You know you have acquired a skill when you can demonstrate the skill given a new problem. Simply stating how it is done is only fact learning. You must do the skill. Furthermore, you must demonstrate the skill given a new problem. Properly punctuating a previously seen sentence would not be evidence of skill learning.

7. When analyzing test errors, determine the error content, type, and source.

8. Successful students regulate learning regularly. They regulate all aspects of their learning from start (getting motivated, selecting key ideas) to finish (analyzing test errors).

Arrange a Successful Study Routine to Help You SOAR

6

Focus Questions

1. Why should you study regularly, not just for exams?

2. Who are the "Lounge Scroungers" and what do they do?

3. What sorts of things tend to grab your selective attention and cause you to become distracted?

4. When should you study for exams?

5. What four things should be included in a block schedule?

6. How should study groups operate?

7. What materials should you study for a test?

8. Why are most students test anxious?

9. How should you prepare mentally, physically, and emotionally for tests?

10. What are some simple ways to diffuse test anxiety?

Surely you remember Roger from Chapter 1. When we last saw him, he had done all sorts of goofy things while studying and was in danger of failing his biology test. Remember? He waited until the night before the test and then tried to pull an all-nighter. He ended up sleeping like a baby on a car ride. Even if Roger had stayed awake, there was just too much material to cram nonsurgically into one brain in one night. Ole Roger also tried studying in the study lounge. That was a waste of time because of all the distractions. He might as well have studied at the airport during a snowstorm. And, remember he studied with a group, but all they did was gripe and exchange useless notes. That was a sharing of ignorance—not knowledge.

Well, Roger failed that test and several others that semester. He left school, told his parents he was studying religion at the Vatican—but had misplaced the phone number—and found work as a night manager at a local laundromat. But when a spin cycle went awry and flooded the place while Roger dozed, he was fired and lost all the jumbo dryer privileges he had amassed.

Now Roger's future hinges on a civil service test used to rank applicants for positions as washroom attendants at the bus station. It's like old times when Roger hits the books on hand-blower repairs and the limitations of low-volume flushers. Roger's had weeks to prepare but doesn't crack a book until the night before. This is the same night his roommate has old friends from Cell Block D over to reminisce. Roger becomes distracted, though, when they pass around crime scene photographs and later exchange contact information about jurors. Roger makes a few calls and heads out to study at a bowling alley lounge with others also hoping to land jobs as bus station washroom attendants.

There, the "study group" bowls a few frames just to jump-start their brains. Any hopes of actually studying, however, end up in the gutter when they accept the challenge of another group of guys celebrating their initiation in an animal waste disposal apprenticeship program. Both good news and bad news come out of this evening. First the good news. Roger averages 176 in his six games and leads his team to victory. Now the bad news. Roger, without sleep and still wearing his rented bowling shoes, goes right from the alley to the test—he fails it miserably. He was underprepared and overanxious. He couldn't even answer the one about whether toilet paper should unravel over or under the roll. His future as a washroom attendant went down the drain. But with each closing door another swings open. Roger is now taking steps toward animal waste.

Okay, okay, none of this really happened to Roger. It's just a jok
mishaps are no joke. Knowing the SOAR study system and how
enough. Effective study skills can be sabotaged by unsuccessfu
Successful studiers also know why, where, when, with whom, ar
And, they know how to combat test anxiety.

WHY YOU SHOULD STUDY

You should study to pass tests or, better yet, ace them. You mi;
"testing game" is rife with problems: "tests are poorly construct
ased against certain cultures"; or "tests tap rote memorization, i
ing." I sometimes agree. I remember pulling a perfect score on a huge statistics test
in graduate school yet being unable to apply statistical ideas to real research problems. Somehow, my study method made me a school success and a real-world failure. Yes, testing has flaws, but schools are not likely to expel the testing institution
soon. Whether or not you condone testing, be ready to play the game.

Testing, however, is not the only game in town. When testing fails to make you
play your best, find other reasons to study effectively and excel. One is achieving
later job success. Suppose your physician, your next airline pilot, or your child's
first-grade teacher had passed the necessary qualifying exams but were unable to
apply the learned information meaningfully. What a frightening thought. Study
your coursework with an eye on future job success so that you can meaningfully
apply ideas in your work setting later. For example, in Chapter 4, you learned how
to create associations. Did you consider how creating associations is useful in your
future job? Physicians create associations to compare and diagnose various dis-
eases. Airplane pilots create associations between wind conditions and landing ad-
justments, and schoolteachers create associations among various categories of
special needs.

When you study for school tests, also keep an eye on how that information can
help you achieve life success. In Chapter 3 you learned how to construct representations. Did you realize that constructing representations can improve your life? In
Chapter 8, you'll see how developing representations can help you make prudent
financial investments and become a millionaire. Wait a minute . . . don't skip ahead!

And let's not overlook the best reason of all to study and learn: learning is interesting and fun in its own right. You've sort of forgotten that haven't you? Before
there was school, you delighted in studying an insect's wings, locating a constella-
tion in the summer sky, reciting a Shel Silverstein poem, playing a melody on the
recorder, and hearing stories about the settling of America. But, when school came
along and began measuring learning with stanines and z-scores, it naturally took
some of the zest out of learning. Don't let that happen. Rekindle the joy. As you

, take time to appreciate the intricacies of the nervous system, the vastness of the cosmos, the wit of a Shakespearean sonnet, the genius of Beethoven, and the spirit of American pioneers. It sounds corny, but now is a golden opportunity for you to learn and enjoy learning. It is unlikely that you will ever again have such an opportunity and the resources to learn. Learn now purely for the sake of learning and cherish the moments.

ercise 1

For each course you are presently taking, think of one good reason for learning that material other than excelling on course tests. I'll get you started . . .

1. English: To find the types of books I'll enjoy reading in the future to myself or my children.
2. Biology: To learn about good training methods for soccer and to learn how to take care of my body as I age.

WHERE YOU SHOULD STUDY

First, let's talk about a few places where you should *not* study. Avoid your bed. There is a high correlation between lying in bed and sleeping—except for two-year-olds. Study in an upright position, making you more alert and less likely to doze. Avoid study lounges. Most study lounges are about 10 percent study and 90 percent lounge. Lounges are full of couches and easy chairs more conducive to resting than studying. They are also full of chatting, coughing, and snoring sounds bound to distract you. Moreover, they are inhabited by "Lounge Scrounges," students who pop in just looking to gab or to lure would-be studiers to a coffee shop or video arcade. Avoid other public places such as libraries, living rooms, and snack bars. Like study lounges, they are frought with distracting movements and sounds.

Second, let's talk a bit about distractions so you understand their danger and how to avoid them. To understand distractions you must understand attention. Your attention operates on two levels. One level is selective attention. Selective attention is whatever you are thinking about or aware of at that moment. It might be this text, a song playing on your CD player, footsteps in the hallway, or a bird flying past your window. Your selective attention is very limited. You can only focus on one of these things at a time. Fortunately, you can shift quickly from one thing to another, for example, from the text, to the song, to the footsteps. Selective attention, then, is much like watching television. You can view only one channel at a time (no picture in a picture here) but can change channels quickly. You have some control over selective attention. You can decide to focus on your text or on your teacher in class. As you'll soon learn, however, selective attention is not always under your control.

The second level is automatic attention. As the name applies, this level of attention happens automatically outside your control. Everything sensed in your immediate environment is attended to automatically—all sounds, movements, tastes, odors, and touches. Unlike selective attention, you are not consciously aware of what's attended to automatically.

Of course, these two levels of attention operate jointly. As you focus your selective attention on this text, or whatever else, many other stimuli in your environment—tapping pens, turning pages, coughs, whispers, lights, and people moving—are attended to automatically. Most things attended to automatically never go any further, but some do. Some grab your selective attention. This is good news and bad news. It is good news because your selective attention can quickly shift from what it's focused on to more important things such as charging tiger (for those reading this along the Serengeti), a crying infant, a news bulletin, a speed trap up the road, and many other important things. It is bad news because your selective attention can also quickly shift from what it's focused on to less important things—distractions. For example, when your focus on reading shifts to whispers, creaking floorboards, and passersby.

You should be wondering now, "What sorts of things being attended to automatically might break through uninvited and grab my selective attention?" Psychologists have researched this question and found that novel things are the biggest culprit. Changes in the environment get noticed. That's why a crashing sound or a shout in the next room gets selective attention. But, so do a barely audible whisper or a creaking door that breaks a silence. They are novel too. Other novelties grab your selective attention when they arise, such as footsteps, chirping birds, a humming engine, a loud commercial with a screaming commentator, or the scent of fresh cut grass.

What does all this mean when it comes to where you should study? It means you need to find study havens virtually free of distractions. Study lounges, snack bars, and libraries are out. A soundproof cubicle is best but perhaps only available if you're a game show contestant. So, find or create the next best thing. When I was in college, I often studied at night in a portion of the library undergoing renovation during the day. I sat on a concrete floor in a vacant hallway. I accomplished more in an hour in that isolated and noiseless hallway than I could in two hours in the library's main room. Another study haven I enjoyed was vacant classrooms. Not many distractions from empty desks and chairs. Find your own private hideaway, perhaps in your room, your closet, or in the garage (without the motor running).

Even small noises can grab your attention.

Wherever you study be sure not to invite distractions. Turn off televisions, computers, radios, telephones, and pagers. Close windows and doors. Even with these measures, though, no place is soundproof (except my children's rooms when I call them for dinner). You can block out occasional noises by using headphones or earplugs, or turning on a fan, which provides a gentle humming sound.

WHEN YOU SHOULD STUDY

Let's discuss first when *not* to study. You should study very little in the three days just before an exam. No, this is not a misprint. Be completely prepared for the exam at least three days in advance—and then relax and just do some light reviewing. This way you'll be less anxious and distractible in the days immediately preceding the exam. It's hard to focus attention when the test is just around the corner. Trying to study the night before the test is like trying to sleep the night before Christmas.

If you prepare at least three days in advance, you will also be less at the mercy of unexpected events. All too often, students get sick, have accidents, or get troubling news from home just before exams, and so they're unable to study as planned. Instructors are usually not sympathetic. They've heard all the variations of the "sick grandmother" story that have ever been invented, and they know that students actually had weeks to prepare.

Now that you know when not to study, let's discuss when you should. Studying should be done throughout the semester on a daily basis. Don't try to cram it all into a few hours or days before the test. The same way that daily running workouts strengthen your body for longer and faster runs later, regular studying strengthens the knowledge and skills that support your additional learning. If you don't exercise regularly, you will not be prepared for more demanding workouts later. Similarly, if you fail to study regularly and stay current in your coursework, you will not be able to grasp new information. The instructor will zoom ahead and leave you in a cloud of dust, gasping for breath, unable to catch up.

Continuing the running metaphor, which is an easier path to meeting your goal of running 90 miles in a month: running 3 miles per day or waiting until the last 3 days and trying to run 30 miles per day? Trying to jam a month's worth of running into three days or a semester's worth of studying into a few nights is a recipe for failure.

The best reason for studying throughout the semester is that there's no reason to wait to SOAR. The first three steps of SOAR should occur regularly throughout the semester. You should select (S) and record complete ideas every day in class and meet with classmates afterward to complete any omissions. You should organize (O) notes by constructing representations at least weekly and create internal and external associations (A) as you do. This way, all that's left to do when you do "study" is to regulate (R) learning. And, even this final stage of studying should occur throughout the semester. Remember to regulate regularly.

Another time-related guideline involves arranging substantial time blocks for studying. As much as possible, arrange to set aside one- to four-hour time blocks for studying. With longer time blocks, there are fewer start-up periods—which include packing books, walking to your study haven, assembling materials, and planning review activities—and a greater likelihood of relating information. For instance, if you're studying about four psychological theories during the same session, you are more likely to note their similarities and differences than if you studied them in separate study sessions days apart.

You can also see the advantages of extended study sessions if you think about them relative to automobile maintenance. It takes less time for a mechanic to change the oil, lube the chassis, rotate the tires, and check the brakes during a single service visit than if she were doing the work over several visits. The mechanic needs to jack up the car only once. She can lube the chassis while the oil drains and remove the tires only once for both rotation and brake inspections. In fact, if she's working on brakes and tires during the same visit, the mechanic is more likely to notice the relationship between the brake's damaged rotor and the tires' uneven wear pattern.

One technique for arranging prolonged study sessions is to develop a block schedule. A block schedule is a guide—not a law—for how you ordinarily spend your days. Exhibit 6.1 provides a blank schedule that you can complete. Exhibit 6.2 shows a sample completed schedule.

Block schedules have four components: classes and commitments, life tasks, study periods, and leisure periods. Each is described next:

1. *Record classes and commitments.* Fill in all class times. Then include ongoing commitments such as work, tennis practice, volunteering, and church meetings. Classes and commitments come first because they are firmly scheduled.

2. *Record life tasks.* Life takes time. Don't deny it; schedule it! Be sure to block out time to handle life tasks such as eating, exercising, showering, washing clothes, cleaning your room, shopping, and keeping appointments. Whenever possible, try to minimize the time needed for these things. For example, exercise first thing in the morning, rather than in the afternoon. You need only one shower instead of two. Fold laundry or iron clothes while enjoying your favorite television program. Answer emails while taking a short study break. Reduce your "lunch hour" to 20 minutes or meet with a study group over lunch. Keep your life in order so you can focus on school and studying when it's time.

3. *Record study periods.* Fill in a sufficient number of study hours (more on what this might be soon). Do not indicate what you will study, however, because this will change from week to week. As already mentioned, try to schedule some larger time blocks of one to four hours. If you schedule much shorter blocks, you'll lose continuity, and studying will become piecemeal and fragmented. Furthermore, you may lose all your study time "warming

EXHIBIT 6.1   *Blank block schedule.*

Block Schedule

	Sunday	Monday	Tuesday	Wednesday	Thursday	Friday	Saturday
6:00–7:30							
7:30–8:30							
8:30–9:30							
9:30–10:30							
10:30–11:30							
11:30–12:30							
12:30–1:30							
1:30–2:30							
2:30–3:30							
3:30–4:30							
4:30–5:30							
5:30–6:30							
6:30–7:30							
7:30–8:30							
8:30–9:30							
9:30–10:30							
10:30–11:30							

EXHIBIT 6.2   *Sample completed block schedule.*

Block Schedule

	Sunday	Monday	Tuesday	Wednesday	Thursday	Friday	Saturday
6:00–7:30		Exercise Breakfast	Exercise Breakfast	Exercise Breakfast	Exercise Breakfast	Exercise Breakfast	
7:30–8:30		Study	Study	Study	Study	Study	
8:30–9:30	Breakfast	History	Study	History	Study	History	Exercise
9:30–10:30	Church	Study	Psych	Campus Errands	Psych	Psych	Breakfast
10:30–11:30	Church	French	Study	French	Study	French	Chores
11:30–12:30	Chores	Lunch	Lunch	Lunch	Lunch	Lunch	Chores
12:30–1:30	Chores	Study	Chem	Study	Chem	Teacher Aid	Chores
1:30–2:30	Lunch	Study	Chem	Study	Chem	Teacher Aid	Lunch
2:30–3:30	Leisure	Study	Study	Study	Study	Study	Study
3:30–4:30	Leisure	Tennis	Tennis	Tennis	Tennis	Tennis	Study
4:30–5:30	Leisure	Tennis	Tennis	Tennis	Tennis	Tennis	Work
5:30–6:30	Supper	Supper	Supper	Supper	Supper	Supper	Work
6:30–7:30	Study	Algebra	Work	Study	Work	Study	Work
7:30–8:30	Study	Algebra	Work	Study	Work	Study	Work
8:30–9:30	Study	Algebra	Work	Church mtg	Work	Leisure	Supper
9:30–10:30	Study	Leisure	Work	Leisure	Work	Leisure	Leisure
10:30–11:30	Bed	Bed	Bed	Bed	Bed	Leisure	Leisure

up," as one college friend did. After repeatedly proclaiming during supper that he had "three hours of studying to do tonight," he often proceeded to take a shower, make some phone calls, fix a snack, listen to some music, and straighten his room before beginning. He was often out of time before he started. If you schedule blocks much longer than four hours, you will become too fatigued to learn. With longer study sessions, remember to include a couple of short breaks (5–10 minutes) hourly to recharge your battery.

4. *Record leisure periods.* Being a student should be fun. As Bluto (John Belushi) put it in the movie *Animal House,* "Being in college was the best eight years of my life." Okay, maybe not that much fun. But, all work and no play is boring and unhealthy. Students who don't find time for fun will surely find time for fatigue and illness. So, be sure to schedule leisure activities. Take advantage of the great opportunities your school and community offer, such as concerts, films, speakers, bicycle paths, and clubs. Learn to play golf or chess. Take up bird watching or Ping-Pong. Find enjoyable activities that recharge your battery for schoolwork.

I'm reminded of a story of two people who chopped wood all day. The first chopped straight through without a break. The second stopped several times and rested. At the day's end, both had a sizable pile of logs, but the second person's was larger. The first person wondered about this and asked the second person, "How were you able to chop more wood?" The second person answered, "Each time I stopped to rest, I also sharpened my ax." Taking breaks to relax and enjoy life will make you a sharper student.

Exercise 2

Complete the blank block schedule found in Exhibit 6.1 by including classes and commitments, life tasks, study periods, and leisure periods.

Returning to the general issue of when you should study, you should recognize that it's also important to take advantage of small time pockets that occur throughout the day. Those spare moments—so often frittered away—are valuable for chipping away at larger tasks and completing smaller ones. For instance, you can use the few minutes before class starts to fix up and fill up notes, organize them, or create associations. You can quiz yourself for an upcoming test while waiting for a medical appointment or a bus. While driving, you can listen to lectures you've recorded. But don't read and drive, especially if you're driving through Lincoln, Nebraska. Time is a precious resource. Don't waste it.

Now to the question: Just how much time should you spend studying? The answer is "a lot." It is hoped that you wish to be a top student. Being a top student—

or a top anything—takes a great deal of time. Take the game of chess, for example. It seems simple enough. There is a board with 64 squares and 32 playing pieces. How hard can this game be? The pinnacle of chess play is becoming a grand master, and researchers have found that it takes, on average, about 50,000 hours of intensive study to become a grand master. That's about 17 years of practice to become one of the game's elite! No one is born a grand master; a person has to earn it.

Why is Tiger Woods so skilled in golf and Mia Hamm so fluid in soccer? The same reason—they dedicate themselves to countless hours of practice. Expertise is made, not born. Expert status is earned through much hard work over a long time period. Emerson said it best: "Every artist is first an amateur."

So, if you want to be a top student, you'll need to do what the experts do and spend a lot of time studying. A good rule of thumb is studying two hours for each class hour. If you're taking 15 hours of classes per week, you should study about 25–30 hours per week. Combine class time and study time and you've got a full-time job. And, that's exactly how you should consider school—as a full-time job, a 40-hour week. As much as possible, then, avoid working during the academic year. Spend your time now earning a good education that will pay dividends the rest of your life.

WITH WHOM YOU SHOULD STUDY

For the most part, studying is a solitary act. Conjure up an image of studying and you will see a solitary figure seated at a desk, poring over stacks of books and papers. The only light comes from a small desk lamp in an otherwise darkened room.

Top students do spend the bulk of their study time working alone, but they also spend substantial time working in study groups, where they share materials, clarify ideas, and test one another on a regular basis. Group study—when done appropriately—is highly effective. In this section, eight guidelines are offered for developing and conducting study groups.

Form a study group for each class. If you are taking math, English, science, and history courses, then form a separate study group for each class that includes members from that class.

Include three to five serious members. Your study group shouldn't be either too big or too small. Too big a group, and responsibility gets sidetracked because members think that someone else will do the work. Too small a group, and the benefits of sharing work and ideas are lost. A study group of between three and five members is ideal.

Include only serious members who pledge to attend all sessions, complete all assignments, and work toward mastering the course. Anyone who cannot make this pledge is more of a hindrance than a help.

Schedule weekly meetings for your study group, and be prepared for study sessions.

Schedule weekly meetings. Begin meeting the first week of the semester and meet regularly throughout the semester. I recommend once-a-week meetings. Don't skip sessions because the next test is weeks away. Cramming is as ineffective for your group as it is for you alone. Your group benefits by completing and sharing work throughout the semester.

Make written assignments. At the conclusion of each session, each group member should be asked to complete a written assignment. Assignments might involve constructing representations, creating associations, or formulating practice tests. Completed assignments are photocopied and shared with your group at subsequent sessions.

Be prepared for study sessions. Study sessions should be a sharing of knowledge rather than a sharing of ignorance. Complete all readings, attend all lectures, and finish all written assignments prior to group meetings. Members should make legible copies of assigned work and distribute them to others in the group.

Stay on task. Your job is to study, not to socialize or gripe about the class. Don't tolerate chatterboxes and complainers. Remember, this is a study group, not a support group.

Be cooperative, not competitive. It is vital that your group cooperate rather than compete. Competition divides and destroys groups. Members should do their best and help others to do their best as well.

It is important not only to act cooperatively and supportively, but also to be honest and up front with one another. When a member's representation is incomplete and disorganized, or his practice test flawed, you should tell him why his work is inadequate. If you don't, everyone in the group will suffer, and the person who produced the flawed work will have no idea that his work needs correction until test time—and by then, it's too late. Further, if group members keep silent because they don't want to hurt someone's feelings, then the group is undoubtedly going to receive substandard work thereafter. Constructive criticism is necessary to improve both individual and group performance.

On the other side of the coin, if you're the person receiving criticism, then recognize its value. Without constructive criticism, your errors will go undetected and uncorrected. Your group's members should not merely tolerate criticism but invite it. Like most medicines, it might not taste good, but it's good for you.

Dismiss noncontributors. Fellow members who don't hold to group guidelines—by skipping meetings, not completing assignments, or behaving uncooperatively—should be asked to leave the group. The group is optional and should only be for those who are seriously committed to it. Agree at the beginning to provide only one warning. If there's a second offense, then drop the person who does not comply. Otherwise, the person will grind your whole group to a halt.

Exercise 3

Based on the study group guidelines, write an informal "contract" that can be signed by all study group members. The contract should specify all the expectations of belonging to and participating in the group.

WHAT YOU SHOULD STUDY

Most students do not have adequate materials to study in preparation for tests. They have sketchy lecture notes, capturing only about 40 percent of the key points. And the entire text chapters that they once read can now scarcely be remembered. If they highlighted the text, they probably highlighted too much, making it difficult now to select the most important text ideas. In short, students have too little information available for study in some ways and too much in others. That's not their only problem. The information is largely unprocessed. That is, students have done little to make sense of it. It's like they have flour, water, yeast, and salt, but they don't have bread. They have not mixed and worked the ingredients into something useful. Their study products and resulting knowledge seem half-baked.

It is hoped that you are no longer like most students. You can use the SOAR techniques to develop excellent study materials that include complete notes, organized representations, internal and external associations, and practice test questions and responses. You'll find these study products and the knowledge they yield fully baked.

COMBATING TEST ANXIETY

"We experience moments absolutely free from worry. These brief respites are called panic."

—Cullen Hightower

Do you shiver at the mention of a test and quake when you take one? When you're taking a test, do your hands tremble, teeth chatter, and head sweat as if you had gulped a jalapeno pepper? Do you encounter mental blocks, surges of panic, or waves of self-doubt? If you experience any of these symptoms, you might have test anxiety.

What Is Test Anxiety?

Test anxiety is a physiological reaction to test situations. The anxious reaction shows itself in many ways, including accelerated heart rate, heavy breathing, blinking, teeth grinding, sweating, fainting, confusion, mental blocks, panic, headaches, crying, and upset stomach.

Before you check in to an anxiety clinic, however, consider this: *classic* test anxiety is rare; perhaps I've met just one or two students with this type of test anxiety in 20 years. In classic cases, the anxiety stems from a genuine fear of tests. This means that *all* tests produce anxiety, even for top students.

Most students instead experience what I call "invited" test anxiety: their anxiousness appears only when they are unprepared for a test. Being unprepared is an invitation for anxiety.

What Should Students Do?

Eavesdrop on any basketball coach readying her team and you'll hear her harp on three types of preparation. "A winning player," she'll say, "is mentally, physically, and emotionally prepared. Mentally, the winning player knows the plays, the opposition's plays, and what to do in any situation imaginable. Physically, the player has become strong and agile. She's rested and properly warmed up. Emotionally, she is fire under control. There's no stress, only nerve. There's no crack in her confidence."

Sound test preparation involves the same three components. The student knows his stuff, he's rested and alert, and he's confident he'll do well. Being mentally, physically, and emotionally prepared for tests gets you ready for success and calms your nerves.

Prepare Mentally

Good mental preparation means knowing your stuff inside and out. Many students never reach this mental level when they study and therefore feel anxious when tested. They should feel anxious—they are woefully underprepared.

Use the SOAR strategies in your mental preparation for tests. Select and note all the important ideas. Organize them using representations whenever possible.

Create internal and external associations. And regulate learning by testing yourself thoroughly before the instructor does. This sort of mental preparation breeds confidence and diminishes anxiety.

Prepare Physically

You're not swimming the English Channel, running the Boston Marathon, or riding a bike in the Tour de France. You're only taking a test. Still, physical preparation is important for reducing anxiety and earning success. Here are a few suggestions for achieving a calm and productive mind-set before a test.

Sound test preparation involves being prepared mentally, physically, and emotionally.

1. **Get a good night's rest.** Tiredness diminishes the brain's performance. When you're tired it is more difficult to concentrate, read with comprehension, perform mathematical calculations, or organize your thoughts. I know the relationship between fatigue and mental ability firsthand: In the early stages of a marathon, I can easily calculate my pace at any mile mark and project my time for later miles. In the later stages of a marathon, I can scarcely add five minutes to my present time.

2. **Eat properly.** When your blood sugar level drops, so does your concentration. When your stomach is empty it writhes and groans, drawing your attention away from the test. Pacify your stomach by eating a nourishing snack or a good meal about an hour before the test. Avoid sweets such as soda, candy, and cake, which provide a surge of energy and soon short-circuit like a string of Christmas lights with a bad bulb. Choose grains, fruits, vegetables, and especially proteins (such as meats and cheeses), all of which have proven staying power.

3. **Exercise.** Light exercise relaxes you and relieves stress. It also wakes up your brain and readies it for the test. While exercising you can also mentally review for the exam. Several world chess champions, such as Bobby Fischer and Garry Kasparov, have relied on daily exercise to relieve tension and help them think clearly.

4. **Choose a good seat.** Part of physical preparation is sitting in a comfortable seat in a location that's relatively free from distractions. In a test environment, every sound is amplified, every movement exaggerated. A sniffle sounds like a

shop vac, a blown nose like a tuba. Students packing up and leaving early take on the proportions of floats in the Macy's Thanksgiving Day parade.

Remember, the best seat for lectures is front and center. That's not a bad location for testing—but you can do better. I recommend a seat away from other students (whenever possible), along a side wall, and away from the door. If possible, angle your seat toward the wall to further block distractions.

Beware, however, of test circumstances that might dictate that you choose another seat. For example, if the proctor invites students to come forward, either with questions or to turn in exams, a seat near the proctor is one that will be chockful of distractions. Exam proctors should (although they don't always) arrange a test environment that is nearly distraction free. If you are distracted by gum chewers, questioners, test completers, or the proctor's conversations, then voice your concern to the proctor and request assistance.

5. Have necessary materials on hand. Take plenty of pencils and pens with you. You need pencils for marking computer sheets or figuring math problems and pens for writing essay responses, and you definitely don't want to be slowed down by a broken pencil or a pen whose ink supply runs out in the middle of the test. Take along scrap paper, too.

Know in advance what other supplies are required or recommended, such as "blue books" for essay responses, a calculator, a ruler, a compass, a protractor, or a dictionary. If the test is an open-book exam, have all allowable reference materials available and clearly marked for easy access. Finally, wear a watch to monitor the time; not all classrooms have clocks or ones that work.

Prepare Emotionally

Professional golfer Shaun Micheel led the prestigious 2003 Professional Golf Association Championship tournament by a single stroke when he was about to hit his approach shot into the 18th green from 175 yards away on the final day of competition. Imagine being in his golf shoes with more than a million dollars in prize money on the line and thousands of spectators lining the course and millions more watching on television. It would be easy to wilt under the pressure—choke on the golf ball–size lump in your throat. Instead, Micheel hit it stiff. The ball arched majestically toward the green, bounced, rolled, and stopped just inches from the cup. An easy tap in and Micheel was the PGA champion.

How did Micheel do it? How does anyone prepare emotionally for important events such as golf competitions, musical performances, or academic tests? Here are some tips.

First, recognize that some nervousness or butterflies are normal and not a bad thing at all. Performance is better at moderate anxiety levels than at low or high anxiety levels, as you can see in Exhibit 6.3. For example, imagine you're

EXHIBIT 6.3   The relationship between anxiety and performance.

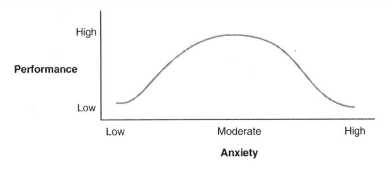

having dinner with your roommate. Your anxiety level might be so low that you could doze off in your clam chowder. Conversationally, you're not at your best. Now imagine you're having dinner with the president and first lady. Your anxiety level might be so high that you could become tongue-tied and so flustered that you would eat your soup with a fork. Conversationally, you're far from your best. Finally imagine you're having dinner with your coach, minister, or favorite instructor. You'd probably display a moderate degree of anxiety that would most likely result in stimulating dinner conversation and appropriate selection of utensils.

One prize example of anxiety's effect is a time students were taking the Scholastic Aptitude Test when a hurricane hit the testing site. Anxiety levels rocketed upward as test takers worried about their homes, transportation arrangements, and loved ones. Examiners figured they might have to throw out the results, given the anxiety-producing conditions. But the test scores turned out to be well above average. The increased anxiety apparently improved performance. This incident suggests that moderate anxiety is good and that students should invite rather than squelch moderate anxiety levels.

Second, recall that the primary source of anxiety is unpreparedness. Students who aren't mentally prepared for a test are naturally anxious. Such anxiety can cripple a student already disabled by inadequate test preparation. Since most test anxiety is the result of unpreparedness, the best solution is to overprepare. Know the information forward, backward, and sideways. Master the information at least three days before the test. Think about the test as "showtime," a time to show off how much you know.

Third, try to duplicate the test situation in advance so that you feel comfortable when the actual test is administered. Prepare several practice tests with study group members. Practice taking the tests under authentic conditions—in a classroom-like setting, with time limits, and without reference materials. Continue the practice tests until you achieve repeated success. This success under simulated conditions breeds confidence that you can succeed under real conditions later.

Fourth, use visual imagery to reduce anxiety and gain confidence. Imagine mildly anxious events, such as having a test announced in class, to severely anxious events, such as not understanding a test question. Replace your panicked reactions with rational reactions by imagining yourself handling the situations confidently. For instance, when there's a test announcement, imagine yourself jotting down the date on your calendar and arranging a study plan that leads up to that day. For a question that you don't understand, imagine seeking assistance from the instructor; calmly rereading the question a second time; or temporarily skipping the item and answering several other items with ease, then returning to the skipped question and answering it successfully. You've probably used mental imagery to overcome the fear of other things—spiders, heights, confined places, public speaking—and now you can use it for tests. In doing so, you replace irrational anxious reactions with the vision of a rational and positive reaction. By practicing the vision, the vision soon becomes reality.

How to Diffuse Test Anxiety

When anxiety does occur before or during tests, there are some surefire ways to defuse it. Following are some examples. Find the way or ways that work best for you:

1. *Take a deep breath.* Deep breaths are anxiety's circuit breaker. When you feel stressed, take a few long, slow, deep breaths, and you'll find you've cut anxiety's power.

2. *Tense and relax muscles.* Anxiety tightens muscles. Show anxiety that its stranglehold on you is weak. Tense affected muscles even more, relax, and feel anxiety release its grip.

3. *Escape to a better place.* The test situation is making you nervous. Take a brief escape by imagining yourself in your favorite safe, calm place. Maybe you're strolling along the water's edge at the beach on a cool fall morning, or watching the sun set over the plains, or reclining in your easy chair in front of a roaring fire. Go there, sit a spell, and come back refreshed and ready to work.

4. *Maintain your perspective.* A test is not a matter of life or death. It's only a test, not a broken leg, lost job, sick baby, or leaking water heater. And, hey, even those things are manageable. When test anxiety creeps in, ask yourself, "What's the worst that can happen?" Be positive. Think to yourself, "I'm healthy and happy and this test result won't change that. I'll do the best I can now and do better next time."

Now get in there like Shawn Micheel, and take your best shot.

Exercise 4

Try practicing the deep-breathing and muscle-tightening defusers. First, imagine a stressful test situation:

You arrive late to class and the other students are hard at work on the test. You glance at the test, expecting to see multiple-choice questions. Instead, you see a single essay. You read it quickly. The question is long, contains many parts, and is confusing. You notice unfamiliar terms. You begin to panic.

Deep Breathing

The purpose of breathing is to get refreshing oxygen into the body. When most people breathe deeply, they expand their chests, lift their shoulders, and gulp in great quantities of air. This sort of breathing is inefficient. It's also not relaxing. Follow these deep-breathing steps to relieve anxiety:

1. Gently blow all the air from your lungs.

2. With your hand across your stomach, inhale gently through your nose as you silently count to four. Feel your stomach expand like a balloon slowly filling with air.

3. Gently exhale most of the air from your lungs. With your hand still gently resting on your stomach, feel your stomach deflate.

4. Slowly repeat the inhaling and exhaling sequence four or five times. Concentrate on the warm relaxing air flowing in and moving throughout your body.

Muscle Tightening

When you're stressed, your body secretes hormones that mobilize your muscles to face a threat. The threat can be real, such as a barking, snapping dog charging at you, or imagined, such as fear or worry about a test.

Much of the tension people carry is visible in their faces, necks, and shoulders. Those lines along the forehead and around the eyes are largely the result of tense muscles. Turn your muscles off when you don't need them. Do you leave your car running in the parking lot while you're at a movie? Of course not. You turn the engine off and let it rest. Follow these muscle-tightening steps to relieve anxiety:

1. Beginning with your face, choose certain muscles, such as those needed to raise your eyebrows, squint your eyes, or clench your teeth, and deliberately tighten the muscles for a few seconds.

2. Release the tension. Feel relaxation sweep over you as you shut the muscle off and let it rest.

3. Repeat this with different muscles, moving down the body until you reach your feet.

SUMMARY

This chapter helped you arrange a successful study routine. Previous chapters told you how to study; this chapter told you why, where, when, with whom, and what to study. It also explained how to combat test anxiety. Why study? Study to earn top grades but also to apply the information meaningfully in your life and future job. Also, learning interesting things is enjoyable. Where to study? Study in quiet and isolated places relatively free of distractions. Otherwise, movements and sounds in your study area will grab your attention. Minimize distractions by clearing them from your environment. For example, turn off telephones and radios. Block out remaining distractions with a fan or headphones. When to study? Study regularly throughout the semester. Don't cram. Arrange for extended, uninterrupted study periods by creating and following a block schedule. Study a lot. There are no shortcuts to success. With whom to study? Study alone but also share your knowledge with a study group and benefit from the members' knowledge. Follow a few simple study group rules: form a group for each class, include three to five members, meet weekly, make written assignments, be prepared for study sessions, stay on task, cooperate, and dismiss noncontributors. What to study? Study the complete notes, representations, associations, and test questions and responses you generate by using SOAR. Overall, studying is not something you do last minute with other unprepared students in a noisy study lounge just to pass a test. Maximize your studying by doing it for the best reasons, in the best places, at the best times, with the best people, and with the best study materials.

Feeling anxious about the upcoming test? Dispel anxiety by preparing mentally, physically, and emotionally for tests. Mentally prepare by using SOAR. Know your stuff. Physically prepare by fueling, resting, and readying your body. A ready body yields a clear mind. Emotionally prepare by practicing and succeeding in both real and imagined testlike settings. Boost your confidence and know that you are prepared for any question and any circumstance that may arise.

ANSWERS TO FOCUS QUESTIONS

1. You should study for exams, of course, but you should also study regularly to best understand the material and be able to apply it in nonschool settings. Also, study for the sheer joy of what is learned.

2. "Lounge Scroungers" are students who hang out in study lounges and distract would-be studiers. Avoid them by studying in out-of-the-way places.

3. Changes in the environment—novelties—tend to grab your selective attention. New things such as a loud cough or a creaking door can easily steal your attention away from a lecture or from studying.

4. You should study early and often in preparation for exams. Cramming is not where it's at. Be prepared for a test at least three days in advance. Studying should be done in extended time blocks during the morning and daytime hours when possible, and also in your spare moments. You should also study a lot. Becoming an expert in anything requires a huge time commitment.

5. In a block schedule include (a) classes and commitments, (b) life tasks, (c) study periods, and (d) leisure periods.

6. You should form study groups for each class. They should include between three and five serious members who meet weekly throughout the semester to exchange and discuss study materials they generate. The group should stay focused, work cooperatively, and dismiss any members who fail to contribute adequately.

7. When studying for a test, study the materials you prepared using the SOAR study system: complete notes, representations, associations, and practice test questions and responses.

8. Most students are test anxious for good reason. They are not mentally prepared for the exam. They do not know their stuff.

9. Prepare mentally, physically, and emotionally for tests. Prepare mentally by using the SOAR study system. Prepare physically by eating, resting, and exercising properly. Also, choose a seat free from distractions and have test materials on hand. Prepare emotionally by recognizing that some anxiety is natural and beneficial, by thinking positively and imagining success, and by practicing in testlike settings to boost comfort and confidence.

10. Test anxiety is easily diffused by doing deep breathing, tensing and relaxing muscles, taking a brief mental escape, and maintaining perspective about the importance of tests.

Harness the Will to SOAR

7

Focus Questions

1. What are the four components of motivation?

2. What are the two origins of desire and which is preferred?

3. What are goal statements and how should they be prepared?

4. What are the four characteristics of good intentions or plans?

5. What are the two characteristics of focus?

6. How should failure be viewed in pursuing one's goals?

7. How should barriers be viewed in pursuing one's goals?

8. Why is it a bad idea for you to believe that success depends on ability?

9. How can you create a bad or good mood for studying?

10. How can you control barriers, such as not finding a parking space on campus or illness, that lead you to miss or be late for class?

I t's over. I'm dead. Make the funeral arrangements," George remarks solemnly to his roommate after attending his first sociology class of the new semester. "No way I'm going to even pass this course," George laments. "The deck is stacked against me." "What's wrong with the course?" George's roommate asks sympathetically. "What's wrong?" George echoes. "Well, let me tell you.

"First, the class meets at 7:30 in the morning. I'm no morning person," George admits wearily. "Classes should never begin before street lights are turned off," he proclaims, as if citing an official ordinance.

"Second, the class meets in Bluemont Hall, clear across campus. I believe that's a toll call from here," he quips. "By the time I trudge over there, I'm late for class.

"Third, the class is huge: there are 300 students. The class outdraws our basketball team," he states ruefully. "I sit way in the back and I can barely see or hear the instructor.

"Fourth, the instructor is *borrr-ing*. He talks like a dentist with a mask on. I've seen statues move more than he does.

"Fifth, the lectures are hard to follow. One minute the instructor's talking about socialization, and the next minute he's talking about sororities and fraternities," he says, rolling his eyes.

"Sixth, the book is as thick as the New York City telephone directory and not nearly as interesting.

"Seventh, I heard the instructor gives true/false tests. I think they're tricky. I'm so gullible that I believe everything I read is true.

"Eighth, I really don't know how I'm going to find the time to study for this class. I have to work 40-plus hours a week to pay for school and cover my auto insurance payments—which just keep climbing," he adds somberly.

"Ninth, I know I'll have trouble concentrating when I do study, having recently broken up with Debbie and Angie," he says dejectedly. "I can't get them out of my mind.

"Last, I just don't like sociology. I mean, what relevance does sociology have for me? When I'm designing buildings with other architects and engineers, we're not exactly going to discuss so-and-so's theory of group dynamics."

"Phew. You're right," George's roommate laments. "You don't have a prayer. I'll round up the pallbearers."

Is George dead (figuratively speaking)? Or, to paraphrase Mark Twain, are reports of his death greatly exaggerated?

George cites several reasons for his impending doom, such as a large class, personal problems, and a dislike for the subject matter. But are these reasons for poor performance, or are they excuses? They sure sound like excuses to me. And, it sure sounds like George has a serious but repairable motivation problem.

THE WILL TO SOAR

You know how to protect the environment by recycling, picking up trash, and conserving resources, but that doesn't mean you will. You know how to keep fit by exercising, eating healthy foods, and getting plenty of sleep, but that doesn't mean you will. And, you, and perhaps George, know how to use SOAR to study, but that doesn't mean you, or George, will.

Knowing how to do something means you have the skill, but getting something done also requires will—the motivation to carry out the skills. Motivated students say, "I will!" In school and in life, you need skill and will. This book has focused on SOAR—important learning skills. Now, we examine the will needed to SOAR to success.

DIFS

Motivation (or will) comprises four factors: **D**esire, **I**ntention, **F**ocus, and **S**ustainment (DIFS). You'll need all four to succeed. Remember DIFS makes the difference.

Increase Your Desire

You've met them: people with little or no desire. They go where the wind blows them. They bob up and down in life's waters. They are pawns—mere foot soldiers—in the game of life. They are cruisers, slackers who don't expect much, do much, or get much.

Then there are those with tremendous desire. They want something badly and thus have a dream—a north star—to guide them. A youngster named Jim Abbott had a dream of playing major league baseball. That's a pipe dream for most youngsters because so few players actually make the big leagues. It was an especially fantastic dream for Abbott, who had only one hand. Abbott's dream, though, was stronger than his disability. Abbott not only made the big leagues; he had a long and distinguished career as a pitcher. He even threw a no-hitter and won a Gold Glove as the best fielding pitcher in the league. Imagine that! It took a lot of hard work for Abbott to succeed, but it all began with a burning desire. Author Ralph Waldo Emerson said, "What lies behind us and what lies before us are small matters compared to what lies within us."

Where Desire Comes From

Desire can come from two places: inside or outside. Inside desire (what psychologists call intrinsic motivation) stems from enjoying the activity. You do the activity because you like it. Outside desire (what psychologists call extrinsic motivation) stems from external rewards. You do the activity because you'll be rewarded for it in some way—perhaps by money or high grades. Although it's best if you have inside desires, both kinds of desire are powerful motivators.

Inside desire. Ideally, it's best if your desires set you on an enjoyable path. As you pursue your dreams, why not enjoy the ride? With inside desire, even if you

Young chess masters play chess because they love it.

never reach your goals, the trip is an enjoyable one. Author Louis L' Amour said, "The trail is the thing, not the end of the trail." Success is in the journey, not the destination.

I have conducted research on young chess masters. Most of these children eat, drink, and sleep chess. They play and study almost constantly. I asked their parents why the young masters work so hard at chess. Every parent echoed basically the same answer: "He just loves it. He just loves playing and studying chess. It's his passion."

I met chess grand master Patrick Wolfe at a tournament in South Dakota and found a moment to speak with him between moves. "I'm an educational psychologist interested in talent and expertise," I blurted out, "and I just need to know how you got here." "I flew out of Boston to Des Moines and took a puddle jumper to Sioux Falls," he replied. After I rephrased my question, he told me that he reached the grandmaster level by waking up every morning at 5:00 as a youngster and studying chess for two hours before school. "Why?" I asked. "Because I loved it and still love it," he said.

Sticking with the chess theme, consider what chess grand master Maurice Ashley says about his chess travels:

I think the process is the most delicious part of the struggle. . . . People set the goal and then don't enjoy themselves while they're doing it. That part of chess, learning about chess, is just fabulous. Relish the moments as you're learning. . . . You have to enjoy the path because otherwise what's the point in what you're doing? It's not about getting to the top of the mountain, it's about climbing. Because when you get to the top, then suddenly you're standing there like "okay, now what?" We don't sit still as humans, we venture and venture and venture. This spirit requires that you enjoy the path as much as you can. . . . For me the process is the joy. (Quoted in Killigrew, 1999.)

The poet Shel Silverstein agrees that the joy is in the venture, the search:

The Search
by Shel Silverstein
I went to find the pot of Gold
That's waiting where the rainbow ends.
I searched and searched and searched and searched
And searched and searched, and then—
There it was, deep in the grass,
Under an old and twisty bough.
It's mine, it's mine, it's mine at last. . . .
What do I search for now?

Copyright © 1974 by Evil Eye Music, Inc.

So what does all this inside desire stuff mean for you—or for George? It means that you should primarily pursue dreams and goals that are enjoyable. Choose paths that wind through enjoyment. Choose majors and courses that interest you. Whenever possible create and pursue projects you enjoy. Participate in activities that are fulfilling. When I was an undergraduate student, I took an educational psychology course and loved it. Consequently, I enrolled in several more educational psychology courses and audited still more. Soon after college, I went to graduate school and pursued an educational psychology doctoral degree. All because I enjoyed the material.

It also means that you should not spend too much time on pursuits that bring you little pleasure. Avoid the trap of chasing a dream that is really not your own. We all know people who go to college (although they hate doing so) to land a high-paying job (they hate) that leads to an even higher-paying job (they *really* hate) that requires them to relocate to a new place (they don't want to be).

I'm reminded of comedian Woody Allen talking about how in his dying moments his life might flash before his eyes. He'd see himself down at the swimmin' hole, fryin' up a mess o' catfish, and gettin' some gingham for Emma Lou . . . when he suddenly realized it was not his life. He was about to die and someone else's life flashed before him. Funny stuff, but with an important message for you: live the life you want to live and enjoy.

Outside desire.   Okay, I'll admit it. I don't like folding laundry, emptying the dishwasher, or cutting the grass. And, I never savored my moments changing diapers. Not every course delighted me like educational psychology. What to do then?

First, recognize that you're not going to love everything you do. You don't like studying for tests or doing taxes? So what. Buck up. You need to do it anyway.

Second, perhaps you can learn to like or appreciate that which seems distasteful. If you, like George, don't like sociology, maybe you can learn to like it. Find out more about it. Read articles; attend lectures; talk to graduate students and professors in sociology who've made this area a career. Find out what they like about it.

Third, consider the benefits of what you're doing. You hate folding laundry but doing so yields a tidy apartment and unwrinkled clothes. You don't like sociology, but learning about it helps you understand family dynamics and what's going wrong in your study group.

Finally, use rewards to create and maintain desire. They work. Imagine if George's rich aunt offered to pay him $1,000 if he aced sociology. Think he could do it? Of course he'd find a way to handle all those *problems*. Large class: Big deal, he'll sit toward the front. Can't concentrate: No problem—he'll record copious notes. That will keep him focused. Dislikes sociology: So what, he need not like it to ace it. In most cases, there is a reward system out there that you can plug into. You can aim for high grades, the dean's list, graduating with honors, or just proving to parents or roommates that you can do it. Or you can build your own reward system. Read a chapter and reward yourself with a video game. Ace a test and buy a new outfit. Pull a 3.0 GPA and go to Padre Island for spring break. And who knows, maybe you'll find enjoyment in the task after all.

Make Goal Statements

Whether your desire stems from inside or outside, you'll need to channel that desire by developing and posting goal statements. Goal statements express your desire. They say what you'll accomplish. Here are a few tips:

Set challenging goals. What are the goals of American youth" Based on what appears in the national media, it seems that society wants its youth to "say no to drugs" and "stay in school." Is this the best our society can do? Are these the goals that dreams are made of? Do you believe these were Albert Einstein's goals as a youth? There is nothing challenging about these goals. "Stay in school?" That's kid stuff. Replace that goal with mastering courses and graduating with honors. "Say no to drugs?" You can do better than that. Say "yes" to developing a healthy lifestyle that includes eating nutritious foods, exercising regularly, getting plenty of sleep, and maintaining a clear mind.

Speaking of Einstein, he admonished his fellow scientists for their meager research goals. He said, "I have no patience with scientists who take a board of wood, look for its thinnest part, and drill a great number of holes where drilling is easy."

Set challenging goals.

As a student, never back down from a challenge. Strive for mastering and earning an A+ in every course. I'm always shocked by the responses I get when I ask students to write down at the start of a semester what grade they expect to earn. More than half report they expect to earn a grade less than an A. Set challenging goals and go after them. Motivational speaker Les Brown (1992) said, "No one ever rises to low expectations."

Set short-range and long-range goals. Okay, you're not exactly sure what you want to be when you grow up. Even a lot of grown-ups still have this problem. It's not unusual, but it's a poor excuse for not setting and pursuing goals. When you're goalless, you wander and may later pay the price for it.

Let me tell you a story about a former student named John. John had worked in a home for troubled youth the past five years and now wanted to pursue a doctoral degree in clinical psychology. This is a rigorous and highly selective field, so I asked John how he had performed in college. "Not very well," he said. "I only had a 2.2 GPA. But I didn't know what I wanted to do back then. I had no goals and I didn't try hard. Now I'm certain that my goal is to become a clinical psychologist and help troubled youth." I had bad news for John. Even his relevant experience and newfound passion might not overcome his weak academic record—not when clinical psychology programs can pick from dozens of experienced and passionate applicants with near-perfect GPAs. John's goalless and largely effortless college career probably slammed the clinical psychology door—and other doors—shut.

While in college, John should have minimally set and pursued some short-range goals such as earning high grades and gaining experience as a research assistant or community volunteer—goals that could serve him well in any future endeavor.

Although setting short-range goals is better than nothing, it is best to set long-range goals too—even if they might change. Here's why. Long-range goals dictate or suggest short-range goals. Suppose your long-range goal is becoming a thoracic surgeon. Naturally, short-range goals then emerge, such as excelling in the required course work, volunteering in a hospital, preparing to take the medical school entrance exam, and finding out what the heck a thorax is. Short-range goals should be the stepping-stones for meeting long-range goals.

Exercise 1

What are your goals? Express your short-range and long-range goals with regard to academics, career, and personal life.

	Goals		
	Academic	Career	Personal
Short Range:			
Long Range:			

Establish behavioral goals. Behavioral goals are observable, measurable. For example, don't say, "I want to be a good writer." This goal is too vague. It doesn't specify the behaviors you demonstrate when the goal is met. A better goal might be, "I will write essays that include topic sentences, more active verbs, better transitions, and correct grammar." These are observable and measurable behaviors.

Behavioral goals are specific. Goals such as studying for one hour are too vague. You can study for an hour and accomplish nothing. Instead, identify your specific activities and the products you'll produce. For instance, you might say, "I will make lecture notes more complete and organized, create associations, and generate and answer practice test questions."

Exercise 2

Change these meager or vague goals to challenging and behavioral goals. I'll get you started.

Meager or Vague Goal	Challenging and Behavioral Goal
1. Review lecture notes.	Master lecture notes using SOAR.
2. Pass Spanish.	Ace Spanish.
3. Take a vacation.	Take a two-week vacation in the Tetons.
4. Get a job.	
5. Take 15 credit hours.	
6. Attend most lectures.	
7. Form a study group.	
8. Organize my life.	

Post or share your goals. You should periodically jot your goals on index cards and then post them on notebooks or above your desk to remind you about your goals. When I began running, I posted the goal statement "sub-three-hour marathon" on the refrigerator to discourage snacking and on my nightstand to boost training motivation for those early morning runs on cold or rainy days. As one final reminder of their desires, many athletic teams post goal statements in the walkways heading out to the playing field. Paul H. Nitze, former Secretary of the Navy, said, "One of the most dangerous forms of human error is forgetting what one is trying to achieve."

You might also share goal statements with supporters—family, friends, teachers—who'll remind you where you're headed if you veer off course, or lend a hand to help you achieve your dreams. Michael Pressley, a great educational psychologist, in talking about his own career success said, "It's much harder to do things on your own, and not as much fun."

My college English professor told me that he once had serious doubts about beginning his doctoral program because he was already 36 years old. He shared his doubts with his father, saying, "It'll take four years to get the degree. I'd be 40 when I graduate." His father offered sage and convincing advice: "The way I figure it, you'll be 40 in four years anyway—with or without your doctorate."

Strengthen Your Intention

Intention means planning to meet the goal. Henry Ford said, "You can't build a reputation on what you are going to do." You've got to go after your goal. And, that starts with good planning.

A runner who desires to run a marathon in less than three hours has to develop and follow a plan that results in a sub-three-hour marathon. For example, the runner plans to run a minimum of 50 miles per week for eight weeks preceding the marathon. Included in that weekly 50-mile total are planned workouts involving a 20-mile run, a hill workout, a run of 10 miles at a 6:30/mile pace, and a run of 5 miles at a 6:00/mile pace.

Academic success depends on intention, too. You need to have a detailed plan for achieving academic success. For example, George's plan for achieving an A on a sociology test might be as follows:

- Attend all lectures and take lots of notes.
- Revise and supplement notes immediately following each class.
- Organize notes using representations.
- Create internal and external associations.
- Generate and answer practice test questions.

The marathon runner and the student need plans to reach their goals. Following are four important considerations involved in good planning.

1. Plan to Succeed

As obvious as this "plan to succeed" advice sounds, some people actually plan to fail or perform poorly. For example, a struggling golf professional was slated to compete in a four-day tournament—Thursday through Sunday. He anticipated he'd play poorly, miss the cut, and be eliminated from the weekend rounds. He was so certain of this fate that he made alternate weekend plans. Good thing. As expected, he played miserably and made an early exit from the tournament.

Don't be a pessimist. Helen Keller said, "No pessimist ever discovered the secrets of the stars or sailed to an uncharted land or opened a new heaven of the human spirit."

Be an optimist. You cannot accomplish what you believe you cannot accomplish. You often can accomplish what you believe you can accomplish. In the 1950s, no runner had ever broken the four-minute mile. Roger Bannister finally broke that barrier. Bannister's record-setting performance tore down the wall barring the four-minute mile. Once runners saw and believed it could be done, several others quickly eclipsed four minutes. Although all were physically capable of breaking the mark before Bannister did, they just didn't believe they could do it.

Believe that you can accomplish your goals. Plan to succeed, not fail.

2. Plan for It to Take a While

"If a man has any greatness in him, it comes to light—not in one flamboyant hour, but in the ledger of his daily work."

—Beryl Markham, English adventurer and author

Suppose your dream is becoming a chess grand master. Suppose too that you have available to you the best chess instruction in the world. You have computer programs, books, and a team of grand masters helping you eight hours a day to learn to play chess. With such high-quality instruction, how long do you think it would take you to attain grand-master status? The answer might surprise you: probably 10–20 years. It is a long road from novice to grand master, and there are no shortcuts. Unfortunately, you can't just pour the vast knowledge of a grand master from his head into yours. You must learn it slowly, move by move, in your own mind.

And, speaking of eminence and time, what do soccer player Mia Hamm, composer Ludwig van Beethoven, chess expert Bobby Fischer, dancer and choreographer Martha Graham, and golfer Tiger Woods have in common? All of them were or are fiercely dedicated to their endeavors, and each person invested incredible amounts of time in their specialties, spending large portions of their life practicing and honing their skills. Another famous golfer, Gary Player, having often heard appreciative fans call out, "Gary, I'd do anything to hit the ball like you," one time shot back, "No, you wouldn't." Player was thinking about his years of practicing in all sorts of weather from morning to night, until his hands could barely grasp the club. That level of dedication is necessary to excel. Though you may not have realized it until now, becoming an effective student also takes considerable time.

An informal survey of freshman students indicated that most were studying less than 10 hours per week, and some were studying only 2 to 3 hours per week. This is not nearly enough study time to excel in school.

Many students don't think learning takes much time. One reason is their belief that expertise occurs naturally, that it's due to innate ability. That's wrong. Experts like Mia Hamm, Bobby Fischer, and Tiger Woods are built, not born. Remember what Emerson said: "Every artist is first an amateur."

Whatever your goals, realize that achieving them will take time and plan accordingly.

3. Plan to Get Started Now

"Slaying the dragon of delay is no sport for the short-winded."

—Sandra Day O' Connor, Supreme Court Justice

The cost of a college education is high now, and projected future costs are astronomical. If your child were born today, how much money do you think you would have to save each month to finance your child's college education 18 years from now? Maybe $10 to $25 a month, depending on the type of college? How about $200 to $400 per month! The point is that the best (and perhaps the only) way to afford a future college education is by getting your investment portfolio started now.

The "get started now" principle is also understandable relative to a new car. Should you wait four or five years after buying a new car before you polish the finish or service the engine? Keeping a new car new requires that you take care of it now.

The point of these questions is, if you missed the opportunity to invest earlier, then invest now. The best time to plant a tree was 20 years ago; the second best time is now.

Early investments in time also aid learning. Too many students procrastinate. One interviewer asked students if they procrastinate. Twelve percent of the students immediately said no, 46 percent said they thought they did, and 42 percent said they'd tell the interviewer later. You should begin assignments and study activities right away. Don't wait for approaching deadlines to get started. If you're assigned 12 chapters to read for the midterm in seven weeks, start reading the first two chapters this week. Studying lecture notes deserves an early start as well. Don't wait until the night before an exam to get started using the SOAR system.

Think about what someone once said: "Procrastination is like a credit card: it's a lot of fun until you get the bill."

4. Plan to Invest Time Regularly

Each day that we awake is a new start, another chance. Why waste it on self-pity, sloth and selfishness?

Roll that day around on your tongue, relish the taste of its freedom. Breathe deeply of the morning air; savor the fragrance of opportunity. Run your hands along the spine of those precious 24 hours and feel the strength in that sinew and bone.

Life is raw material. We are artisans. We can sculpt our existence into something beautiful, or debase it into ugliness.

—Cathy Better, in the Reisterstown, Maryland, *Community Times*

Nearly every day you should be investing time toward achieving your goals. If you want to be a writer, you should be writing regularly.

Regular investments—even small ones—pay off. Do you like to read? How would you like to read 15 or 20 novels every year in addition to your textbooks? It sounds impossible, doesn't it? But in order to read that many books in a year, all you need to do is read for 15 minutes before bed each night.

Many of my colleagues complain that they don't have time to stay current in their field by reading professional journals. But if they read just one journal article every night (requiring about 20 minutes), five days a week, they would complete 250 articles per year. In four years, they would read 1,000 more articles than the person who believes there isn't enough time to stay current.

Investing regularly not only produces more learning; it produces *better* learning. Consider the cases of John and Jan. John studies his lecture notes for 20 minutes after each class. Each week, he spends an hour integrating his class notes for that week. During the week before his midterm exam, he studies an extra hour every day. In total, John studies about 20 hours for the exam. Jan, however, does not begin to study until two days before the exam. She studies 10 hours each day, and she, too, has a total of 20 hours of studying.

What are the likely outcomes for John and Jan? Before you answer, consider John and Jan's approaches relative to another area. Suppose that both wish to improve their cardiovascular fitness by running. They set as their goals running 90 miles per month. John runs 3 miles every day for a month. Jan doesn't get started until the last three days of the month. Even if she were to run 30 miles each day over the next three days (very unlikey, even for a seasoned runner), would she benefit as much as John?

The answer is no. Each day, a little at a time, John builds a higher level of muscular and cardiovascular fitness. Thus, his running improves throughout the month, because each day he is capable of running more effectively. Jan, on the other hand, cannot possibly attain the same fitness level with three days of running, regardless of the number of miles she runs. In fact, her attempt to run 30 miles in one day is likely to do nothing more than leave her sore and tired.

The same is true regarding their study behaviors. By studying each day, John "stays up" with the instructor. He can understand new lecture material better than Jan. Even studying for 40 hours before the test might not help Jan if she cannot understand her lecture notes, which she never reviewed before. By not studying regularly, Jan simply cannot bring a sufficient depth of knowledge to her late studying efforts. Furthermore, Jan's marathon study sessions are likely to leave her tired and poorly motivated.

Plan to make regular time investments toward achieving your goals.

Exercise 3

Select one of the goals you set earlier and make a plan for achieving that goal. Keep in mind the four aspects of good planning: plan to succeed, plan for it to take a while, plan to get started now, and plan to invest time regularly.

Focus Your Effort

Focus has two components: hard work and staying on track.

Work Hard

Harvard psychologist Howard Gardner examined a group of talented individuals and showed that creative ideas or products are the result of hard work over a long period of time—usually 10 to 20 years. Albert Einstein toiled in physics for more than 10 years before offering his breakthrough contribution on relativity. Even the prodigious Wolfgang Amadeus Mozart, who began his musical career at age 6, did not create a magnificent composition until he was 16—10 years later. Success as a scientist, an artist, a composer, or a student requires hard work. Consider what author Sarah Brown said: "The only thing that ever sat its way to success was a hen."

Focused individuals work hard to follow their plans and reach their goals. Many students don't realize this. They look at outstanding individuals such as Mozart,

Marie Curie, Pablo Picasso, Sigmund Freud, dancer Martha Graham, Einstein, or former chess champion Bobby Fischer, and they believe that those people possess God-given talent that springs forth in a shower of inspiration. Freud scoffed at that notion. He said, "When inspiration does not come, I must go halfway to meet it."

Author Jeffrey Archer captures the importance of hard work. He says "Never be frightened of those you assume have more talent than you do, because in the end energy will prevail. My formula is: energy plus talent and you are king; energy and no talent and you are still a prince; talent and no energy and you are a pauper."

Stay on Track

> "No steam or gas drives anything until it is confined. No life ever grows great until it is focused, dedicated, disciplined."
>
> —Harry Emerson Fosdick, theologian and writer

Because reaching your goals requires maximal time and effort, don't waste too much time getting off track—doing things inconsistent with your goals. Psychologist Mihaly Csikszentmihalyi studied highly productive individuals and found that they focused hard on their work and commonly ignored things that got in the way of completing their work. They didn't allow themselves to be spread too thin. As a case in point, Csikszentmihaly (1996) received this reply from one highly productive individual asked to participate in the study:

> I hope you will not think me presumptuous or rude if I say that one of the secrets of productivity is to have a VERY BIG waste paper basket to take care of ALL invitations such as yours—productivity in my experience consists of NOT doing anything that helps the work of other people but to spend one's time on the work the Good Lord has fitted one to do, and do it well. (p. 14)

Check periodically to see if you're on track. A colleague of mine recently did just that. He made two lists. The first listed his goals and priorities. The second listed how he spent the bulk of his time. He saw immediately that the two lists were at odds. He was not doing things or enough things consistent with his goals and priorities. For example, he highly valued religion but spent little time fostering that value. He wanted to write a book but was scarcely spending any time working on it. He valued fitness but rarely worked out. He noticed a lot of time drainers inconsistent with his goals and priorities. There were countless committee meetings, a lot of wasted travel time, and even a lot of television viewing. As a result, he opted off several committees that were not of interest, used travel time to dictate notes for his book, and restricted television viewing to 30 minutes per day. He took hold of his life and better focused his efforts. He put his time where his goals were.

To be focused, you need not be one dimensional. You can pursue multiple goals—especially when those goals are compatible. I interviewed top educational psychologists to determine the secrets of their success. Michael Pressley, one of the three most eminent educational psychologists, revealed that his secret is focused integration. Many professors teach a set of courses, conduct research, and serve their profession as if those were three distinct and separate jobs. There is little connection among their teaching, research, and service. Not so for Pressley. He masterfully integrates the three. For instance, his research interest was strategy instruction, so he taught a course on this topic. Then, he and his students conducted more research on strategy instruction and coauthored a strategy instruction textbook to serve educators. Rather than be pulled into several disjointed areas, Pressley focused his efforts on integrated goals.

Focused integration has implications for life decisions as well. Wanting to earn a million dollars and wanting to be a schoolteacher are probably incompatible goals. Wanting to teach school and wanting time to spend with family are compatible or integrated goals.

To sum up, work hard to achieve your goals. And, stay on track. Don't get derailed by things unrelated to your goals.

Exercise 4

1. Reexamine the goals you set earlier. Is there focused integration? Do the goals complement each other or do they send you in opposing directions? Specify how they complement or compete.
2. What things take up a lot of time in your life but are not really fun or leading you to your goals? Consider how you might reduce or eliminate them.

Sustain Your Effort

"Let me tell you the secret that led to my goal. My strength lies solely in my tenacity."

—Louis Pasteur, scientist

Motivation must be sustained. How many people do you know who quit smoking—five times? Or who go on and off diets on a monthly basis? These people have trouble sustaining their motivation and performance.

Sustaining motivation produces remarkable results. Remember that the tortoise defeated the hare by sustaining motivation, and that a steady trickle of water moves mountains while intense earthquakes and hurricanes produce little long-term effect. Consider, too, baseball pitcher Nolan Ryan, the career strikeout leader, who pitched in the major leagues for more than 25 years. While his contemporaries participated in "Old-Timers" games, Ryan threw his eighth no-hitter at age 44. Ryan attributed his longevity and success to keeping in top shape throughout his career. He trained hard every day to sustain his remarkable physical conditioning.

Consider what another world-class athlete, former American miler Jim Ryun, said: "Motivation is what gets you started. Habit is what keeps you going." So create good habits. Author Colleen Mariah Rae said, "Good habits are just as hard to break as bad ones."

Similarly, a student who plugs away—registering perhaps only small gains—throughout the semester and throughout college is likely to accomplish a great deal. My former graduate adviser at Florida State University offered a single piece of advice each time he met with a student: "Stay with it now," he would invariably say before he and the student parted. "Stay with it now." What a great piece of advice! It means that no matter how difficult or impossible things become, you just stay with it. You keep plugging away and never, ever give up.

Of course, it's easier to stay with something if you enjoy doing it. Take my friend who works as a guide in the Rocky Mountain National Park, leading long hikes six days a week. On her day off, you might think she sleeps in, soaks her bunions, and puts her feet up. Nope. She hikes. It's what she loves to do.

It is hoped that it is the joy of learning that will sustain you throughout school, not just the desire to achieve high grades or receive awards and diplomas. School is tremendous fun for those who know how to learn and are willing to sustain the effort.

Sustaining effort—maintaining positive habits—is not always simple in the face of failure and other barriers. Let's take a look and see what you might do.

Confront Failure

"There are no secrets to success. It is the result of preparation, hard work, and learning from failure."

—General Colin L. Powell

You *will* fail. Everyone fails, even the great ones. Ty Cobb was one of the greatest hitters in baseball—a lifetime .367 hitter. But that means Cobb failed to get a hit more than 6 out of every 10 times he batted. Author F. Scott Fitzgerald once had 122 rejection slips pinned to his walls. Michael Jordan was cut from his high school basketball team. And, how about this record of ineptitude (his age appears in the right-hand column):

Failed in business	22
Ran for legislature—defeated	23
Again failed in business	24
Suffered nervous breakdown	27
Defeated for elector	31
Defeated for Congress	34
Defeated for Congress	39
Defeated for Senate	46
Defeated for vice president	47
Defeated for Senate	49
Elected president of the United States	51

Can you guess whose record this is? It is that of Abraham Lincoln.

So there is no question that you will fail, just as all of these individuals did at one time. The question is, "How will you react to failure?" Les Brown says, "It doesn't matter what happens to you, only what you'll do about it." Chess grand master Maurice Ashley has this to say about losing:

> Some people lose a horrible game and they can't forgive themselves. Then the rest of the tournament is colored by the fact that they lost that bad game instead of saying, "okay, that's life," and move on . . . boy, do you have to get used to losing. . . . It's not that a competitor enjoys losing, or doesn't lose, it's that a competitor continues to compete despite having lost. The best competitors are those who don't become demoralized by a loss, they become energized by it. That's the trick. Look at (former World Champion) Garry Kasparov. After a loss, invariably he wins the next game. He just kills the next guy. That's something we have to learn to be able to do. (Killigrew, 1999)

Harvard psychologist Howard Gardner studied outstanding creators and found that they all shared a common virtue called framing. All were able to frame their defeats and failures in positive ways. They saw failure not as an end but as an opportunity to learn, grow, and try again. They saw occasional failure as the price of improvement. Consider, for example, the Wright Brothers' invention of the flying machine. This machine was not invented in one grand attempt. Instead, the brothers failed dozens of times over five years, each time making slight improvements as they learned from their failures.

Writer James Michener equates framing with character. He said, "Character consists of what you do on the third or fourth tries."

Overcome Barriers

As you sail through life's waters following your north star, there will be troubled waters—maybe fierce storms and turbulent seas. Faced with such barriers, you can abandon ship or find the courage and means to sail onward. On the sea, in school, and in life, there are always barriers. To realize your goals, you'll need to sustain your effort and overcome whatever barriers await you. Publilius Syrus, who wrote in the 1st century B.C., said, "Anyone can hold the helm when the sea is calm."

Remember George from the beginning of this chapter? He faced all sorts of barriers he thought would doom him in sociology. The class was too large, lectures were hard to follow, the class was boring . . . So what! What George and you must do is stop making excuses and find ways to deal with such barriers. Cartoonists Don Wilder and Bill Rechin said, "Excuses are nails used to build a house of failure."

Let's see what strategies might be used in response to some common school barriers.

"I lack ability." This barrier comes in many flavors such as "I'm stupid," "I'm not good at math," or "I'm lousy at sports." This belief is flawed. The truth is, your performance is based largely on your learned skills and your motivation: skill and will beat inborn ability every time. The "I lack ability" belief is also problematic because it leads students to dismiss the help that skill and will might provide. Students who attribute their poor school performance to low ability are cold to skill and will remedies. If their teachers say, "I have some great note-taking strategies to help you learn," they think, "I have low ability. I can't learn those strategies." If teachers say, "You need to put forth more effort," they think, "More effort won't help me. It's a waste of time. I'm dumb."

The flipside is equally wrong and detrimental. Students who believe they have high ability think, "I don't need to learn note-taking strategies, because I have a great memory. I'll remember all of this without writing it down." And they think, "I don't need to put more effort into my schoolwork. I have high ability."

You must remember that your performance is the result of skill and will, not innate ability. Don't abandon your dreams because you think you lack ability.

"I'm not in the mood to study."

> "A professional is someone who can do his best work when he doesn't feel like it."

> —Alistair Cooke, journalist and broadcaster

Many students believe that their moods are outside of their control, when, in fact, students put themselves in the mood for not studying. They actually develop plans for doing so. Want proof? Record five plans that you use for not being in the mood to study.

Perhaps you recorded some of the following plans for creating a bad mood:

- studying late at night
- studying where it is noisy
- studying when friends are going out for the night
- studying six chapters at one time
- studying alone
- studying when a favorite television program is on
- studying just to get a high (or passing) grade

All of these plans are conscious choices. You could just as easily make choices that create a positive mood for studying, such as

- studying in the morning or between classes, when you're more alert
- studying in a quiet location, such as a study carrel in the library
- studying before friends go out for the night
- studying a chapter a week, rather than six at once
- studying in a group, rather than alone
- studying now and watching a favorite program on videotape later
- studying to learn, rather than just to get a high (or passing) grade

Most likely the main reason for students not being in the mood to study is that they're not sure *how* to study. And without instruction in how to study, many students use ineffective and passive strategies such as RE-reading, RE-copying, and RE-citing. As I stated before, such strategies are RE-diculous. Now that you've learned SOAR, use those techniques to put you in a better mood to study.

"The class is boring." Classes are not boring. Boredom is a choice you make. If you find that a lecture isn't stimulating, there are several choices you can make to combat boredom. During the lecture you can record a complete set of notes. Recording complete lecture notes requires attention and is incompatible with boredom.

Lectures can also become more interesting if you make comments and ask questions of the instructor throughout the lecture. Reading more about the topic, particularly in advance of the lecture, also makes the lecture seem more interesting. After the lecture, you can speak with the instructor or fellow students to learn more about the topic.

Texts aren't boring either. You can choose to become bored while reading them. Some of the strategies you can use to aid your text comprehension and thereby reduce boredom include constructing a quality set of notes, organizing ideas, creating associations, and generating and answering questions. When you listen and read actively, you cannot be bored.

The "I'm bored" excuse is remindful of children with a room full of toys and books who squawk, "I'm bored," or of adults who seek artificial thrills through drugs or other indiscretions because they are bored. I side with Professor of American Studies Toni Flores, who says, "The world is full of wonders, riches, powers, puzzles. What it holds can make us horrified, sorrowful, amazed, confused, joyful. But nothing in it can make us bored. Boredom is the result of some pinch in ourselves, not of some lack in the world."

Ask yourself: Just how sick am I?

"I don't feel well." Some students allow an illness to stand in the way of reaching their goals, and others do not. Consider the cases of Amy and Jennifer. One night, Amy arrived early as usual for her three-hour night class. As I spoke with her, it was evident that she had a miserable cold and a hacking cough. I said, "You're sick as a dog. What are you doing here?" Amy sneezed and replied in a throaty whisper, "I hate to miss tests." "Okay," I mumbled, covering my mouth, "go sit way over there away from me." Amy completed the test during the first hour of class. Afterward, I asked her how she felt. "Lousy," she said, "but I'm going to stick around for the lecture now anyway. I hate to miss lectures." The other student, Jennifer, left immediately after the test. She complained that she was catching a cold and thought it best to go home and rest. Their test scores reflected their outlooks more than their illnesses. Amy scored a 97 and Jennifer a 75.

By all standards, Amy was very sick and should have stayed home, but she wasn't going to allow her sickness to block her commitment to class and learning. Jennifer, who was not very sick, let her illness become an obstacle.

Motivated students don't let illnesses prevent them from doing their jobs. First, ask yourself if you could make it to class. Try asking the question this way, though: "If I had tickets to a Broadway play, if I were in the finals of the U. S. Open tennis championships, if I were getting married . . . could I make it?" Or, are you like Peggy Ann McKay in the Shel Silverstein poem, who feels dreadfully sick only when she thinks it's a school day?

Sick

by Shel Silverstein

"I cannot go to school today,"
Said little Peggy Ann McKay.
"I have the measles and the mumps,
A gash, a rash and purple bumps.
My mouth is wet, my throat is dry,
I'm going blind in my right eye.
My tonsils are as big as rocks,
I've counted sixteen chicken pox.
And there's one more—that's seventeen,
And don't you think my face looks green?
My leg is cut, my eyes are blue—
It might be instamatic flu.
I cough and sneeze and gasp and choke,
I'm sure that my left leg is broke—
My hip hurts when I move my chin,
My belly button's caving in,
My back is wrenched, my ankle's sprained,
My 'pendix pains each time it rains.
My nose is cold, my toes are numb,
I have a sliver in my thumb.
My neck is stiff, my voice is weak,
I hardly whisper when I speak.
My tongue is filling up my mouth,
I think my hair is falling out.

My elbow's bent, my spine ain't straight,
My temperature is one-o-eight.
My brain is shrunk, I cannot hear,
There is a hole inside my ear.
I have a hangnail, and my heart is—what?
What's that? What's that you say?
You say today is . . . Saturday?
G'bye, I'm going out to play!"

Copyright © 1974 by Evil Eye Music, Inc.

Second, if you must miss school because of illness or some other reason, then take steps such as the following to be sure you don't miss material:

Quick Tips if You *Must* Miss Class

- Arrange for a friend to videotape the class.
- Arrange for a friend to audiotape the class.
- Arrange for friends to lend you their detailed notes.
- Ask fellow students questions about the class.
- Ask the instructor for reading materials related to the class.

Speaking of "other reasons" why you must miss class, most reasons don't hold water. For example, one of my students was a basketball player. He missed two consecutive classes because his ride didn't show up. "That's no excuse," I told him. "What would you do if your ride didn't show up to take you to a game?" He had no trouble coming up with solutions then, such as calling a teammate, the coach, or a taxi for a ride; riding his bike; or walking. "Yes," I said, "You can do all those things for class too. Heck, you can dribble to class." Exhibit 7.1 provides other excuses students make for missing class and their potential solutions.

"The class is too large." Some classes enroll more people than are in some students' hometowns. Large classes can be intimidating and impersonal, but they don't need to be "too large" for you. You can do several things to make a huge class seem more personal and comfortable. First, sit toward the front, where there are fewer distractions between you and the instructor. This way, you can establish eye contact with the instructor and get the impression that he or she is speaking directly to you.

Second, ask questions and offer comments. Most instructors welcome student participation in the discussion—even when the class is large. Your participation shows instructors that you are interested. Remember, too, that this is your education and you're paying for it. Be assertive. Don't be afraid to speak up if you have something to contribute.

EXHIBIT 7.1   Sample excuses and solutions.

Excuses	Solutions
"My ride didn't show up."	Find more dependable friends. Call a taxi. Run. Would you leave your fiancée at the altar because your ride to the church didn't show up?
"I couldn't find a parking space."	There were probably several spaces available at 7:00 A.M. Park early in the day, when spaces are available, or park off campus and walk. Use public transportation. Ride your bicycle. Would you miss a concert that you paid for because you couldn't find parking nearby?
"I had to work for a friend."	Did the friend force you to do so? Tell your friend that you have a prior commitment to attend class. Would you work for your friend when you have expensive tickets to a play?
"I had to pick up my grandmother at the airport."	Ask your grandmother to wait until your classes are finished. Arrange for a friend to chauffeur her. Order a taxi, bus, or limousine for her. Grandma will respect your commitment to school and probably slip you a few bucks in support of it. Would you run off to pick up Grandma during a job interview?
"I overslept."	Use multiple irritating alarm clocks, placing one across the room. Arrange for a wake-up call. How long would you remain employed if you overslept while working in a large corporation or as a teacher?

Finally, be mentally active. In your mind, try to answer the instructor's questions, raise your own questions, and think about what the instructor says. Look for relationships among presented ideas (internal associations) or how the ideas relate to your background knowledge (external associations). Evaluate the merit of the ideas that the instructor presents. Mental activities like these keep you tuned to the lecture despite the large class size.

"The class is too early." If you were out in the real world and you tried telling your boss or your drill sergeant that you weren't a morning person, it is extremely doubtful that either would be sympathetic.

Avoid blaming poor performance on scheduling factors that are controllable. If you prefer sleeping in, try to arrange to take classes later in the day. When you must take classes earlier, adapt your schedule. Going to bed earlier is one good way to overcome the early class problem. Getting up early to exercise and eating a healthy breakfast (think of this as brain food—because that's what it is!) before your first class might also put you in a positive frame of mind. B. F. Skinner, the noted behavioral psychologist, got up at 4:00 A.M. each day and wrote until 7:00 A.M., a time when most people are just rising. This early morning period was the most productive part of Skinner's day. Who knows, maybe you'll find you're a real dynamo in the morning.

"I have a personal problem." As a student, you will probably experience personal problems that range from being physically challenged to having an ailing family member to having a wrenching breakup with a partner. You might find yourself thinking about your problem while you're sitting in English class, or maybe reading a history textbook, or trying to study for a biology exam. The problem distracts you, and you might begin to think that the problem is the direct cause of ineffective study behaviors and poor academic performance. However, letting a personal problem distract you is a choice *you* make.

I am not suggesting that personal problems are unimportant. Not true. They are very important. However, effective students have strategies for isolating the problem and dealing with it at appropriate times. For example, you might put aside time to meet with a counselor or talk with a partner when doing so does not interfere with class attendance or studying. You might record thoughts and feelings in a journal as they occur and think about them later that evening. Maybe you'll set aside time to do mind-refreshing exercises or to throw darts at a picture. History is filled with people who had awful personal problems but nevertheless achieved great success. For example, President Franklin D. Roosevelt was badly crippled by polio and confined to a wheelchair—but that didn't stop him from becoming one of the greatest presidents we've ever had. The point is, people like Roosevelt don't allow personal problems to interrupt their work.

"The test was unfair." Have you ever attributed a bad grade to an unfair test? Tests often do contain poor items that are too difficult, fail to discriminate between those who know and do not know the content, or fail to correspond to course objectives. Instructors should ignore these items when they evaluate student performance. However, students who blame their poor performance on the test or how it's scored probably won't improve their test preparation for the next test.

Students who perform poorly on tests often blame the instructor and then display hostility toward the instructor. This is evident when the student challenges every test answer that was marked wrong. The student becomes offensive and repeatedly whines, "Why did I get this wrong?" or "Why wasn't my answer right?" The student isn't interested in understanding why an answer was wrong, only in challenging the instructor.

Brooding over poor test performance, which they attribute to teacher unfairness, leads some students to cut class, retreat to the back of the room, sit sideways in their chairs with arms folded, or stop listening and taking notes. You can sometimes see steam coming out of their ears. These behaviors are counterproductive. There is no way that acting like this can lead to better performance on the next exam. Even if a test is unfair, don't make choices likely to result in even lower test performance on the next exam. Most important, analyze your test errors, determine their source, and take productive steps toward correcting them.

Blaming poor course performance on the instructor's grading policies is also futile. For example, a student who has a 69 average and receives a D in the course might contend that the grade should be a C, since it was only one point shy of a C average. The student blames the instructor for giving a low grade. Students must realize that instructors do not give grades; they assign them based on a student's academic performance. Instructors don't choose grades; students do. Students can choose to earn an A or an F. The student who received a D chose to earn test scores that averaged less than 70 percent.

The tendency to blame somebody or something else for poor performance is often seen in sports. When a team loses, the officials get blamed. Consider the following situation: With five minutes left in the game, a basketball official calls a fifth and final foul on the team's star player. The player leaves the game with her team trailing by one. A videotape of the call indicates that the player did not foul—that the call was wrong. The team goes on to lose by three points. Afterward, the coach is livid and berates the official who made the bad call. The coach blames the official for the loss.

Now examine the "stats" for the losing team: 21 turnovers, 32 percent shooting from the field, 8 for 15 from the free-throw line, and outrebounded 48 to 62. You decide whether the bad call was the reason for the loss. Don't forget that the star player had four previous fouls and that the team was trailing at the time the fifth foul was called.

This is not to say that instructors are always right and students are always wrong. The point is that students need to identify the real source of their poor test or course performance. They need to take steps toward improving performance next time, usually through better study methods. The same is true for the basketball team. The players need to improve their deficiencies. Blaming the referee will not produce any improvement in the team. Employment guru Robert Half said it well: "The search for blame is always successful."

Exercise 5

> Return to the scenario involving George at the beginning of the chapter. Have a talk with George and let him know why each of his 10 "reasons" for failing sociology is an excuse. Give him strategies in each case to hurdle the barrier.

SUMMARY

Poor academic performance is the result of using ineffective strategies (poor skill) and having insufficient motivation (poor will). It is not the result of factors such as boredom, problems with a boyfriend or girlfriend, large classes, or illness. These are excuses. Effective students overcome barriers to learning. They use effective strategies and they maintain motivation. Motivation is the result of Desire (setting goals), Intention (planning), Focus (working hard and staying on track), and Sustaining effort (despite failures and barriers). DIFS makes the difference. It's up to you to control these factors and SOAR to success. Just do it!

ANSWERS TO FOCUS QUESTIONS

1. The four components of motivation are desire, intention, focus, and sustainment (DIFS). Desire is wanting to accomplish a goal. Intention is planning how to reach that goal. Focus is staying on track and working hard at accomplishing that goal. Sustainment is continuing to work toward that goal over a long period of time despite failures and barriers that arise.

2. Desire can originate from *inside* a person, which means he wants to do something because he enjoys the process. Desire can also originate from *outside* a person, which means she wants to do something because she gets some tangible reward such as a grade, money, or a trophy. Inside desire is preferred because a person works best when pursuing a goal or dream that's personally meaningful and fun to pursue.

3. Goal statements are written statements that express your desire. The statement should express challenging goals written in behavioral terms. The goal statement, "I want to improve in golf," is neither challenging nor behavioral. It's unclear how improvement is to be measured and, as written, any improvement meets the goal. A better goal might be, "I want to hit my driver 250 yards consistently and lower my average score by five strokes." Goal statements should also reflect both short- and long-range goals, where the short-range goals are steps to meeting long-range goals. Goals should also be posted or shared to remind you where you are headed and to enlist the support of others.

4. Good intentions or plans have four characteristics. First, plan to succeed. Believe you will succeed. Second, plan for it to take a while to reach your goals. Reaching most goals requires a sustained effort. Third, plan to get started now. There is no time like the present. To wait is to waste time. Fourth, plan to invest time regularly to meet your goal. Regular time investments pay off.

5. Focus means working hard toward your goals and staying on track—not wasting too much time on things unrelated to your goals.

6. When pursuing your goals, expect failure; embrace it. It's bound to happen and it provides you with information helpful in achieving your goals. Everyone fails. The key is how you handle it.

7. There are always going to be barriers to your goals. You must find a way over, through, under, or around them. Don't let them stop you. For every barrier there are strategies—under your control—for overcoming the barrier.

8. Believing that success depends on ability is a dangerous barrier because if you think you have either low or high ability, you're not likely to use strategies (skill) or spend more time (will) trying to improve your academic performance.

9. You can create a bad mood for studying, for example, when you try to study at times when you prefer to do other things such as sleeping, visiting friends, or watching television. You also can create a bad mood by studying under difficult conditions, such as in a noisy study lounge. You can create a good mood for studying, for example, by studying when your mind is fresh, when you are rewarded, where you can concentrate, and when you use effective strategies.

10. The parking problem is handled by coming to school early in the day, when many parking spaces are empty. Or you can walk to school, ride your bike, take a bus, or ride with a friend. If you're ill, ask a classmate to record the lecture or lend you notes. Most factors that *cause* you to miss class or be late can be overcome.

SOAR Applications

8

Overview

Focus Questions

1. What is the main difference between lecture and text learning with respect to SOAR?

2. During lectures, students select important information by recording it in notes. How else can students select information when learning from text?

3. With what does almost all writing begin?

4. How do the SOAR components relate to writing?

5. Beyond school, how might SOAR be used to solve problems in the real world?

6. How might SOAR help you become wealthy?

An Interview with Roger, Reprinted from *Animal Waste Digest*

Reporter: Roger, you've just won the Bronze Scooper for outstanding contributions to waste. It's been widely reported, though, that you were not always the Wizard of Waste you are today. Tell us what life was like before walking down this path.

Roger: Well, it was a lot easier to keep my shoes clean. Ha, ha, just a little trade joke. I was a total slough throughout my college career—all three months. I'd wait until the night before tests to study. Then, I'd read and reread my pathetic notes—there weren't enough pages in those notes to paper-train a spider. My grades stunk worse than a fox's den, if you know what I mean. After college, I even failed a civil service test for becoming a washroom attendant. That career hope went down the drain. It's funny, though, how when one stall closes another one opens. I happened to meet folks entrenched in animal waste. Before long, I jumped in with both feet.

Reporter: How'd you make such a big splash?

Roger: It all began with bird droppings. My first job was at a pet store cleaning bird cages. I was using old notebook paper from my college notebooks to line cage bottoms when I came across some of my old notes from a study skills class I attended when it didn't interfere with holidays like Flag Day and Groundhog Day. Anyway, the notes were about a study skills system called SOAR.

Reporter: How did they help?

Roger: Well, the notes told how to study and get motivated. "What a gas," I thought, "I can use this stuff to become an animal waste expert and maybe leave my mark in the field." And, it came to pass.

Reporter: How did SOAR help exactly?

Roger: Well, according to SOAR, first you have to select and note all the important content—that's *S*. So, I got my hands on all the animal waste reports I could. I scooped up all the important ideas and made notes. Then I organized the notes in piles—that's the *O* in SOAR.

Next, I needed to make associations—that's the *A* in SOAR. So, after constructing a waste matrix, I started to sniff out all the similarities and differences (internal associations) among waste types. Oddly, very few in the scientific community were nosing around this stuff.

	Then I made external associations. I started thinking outside the litter box, so to speak. I started thinking about other wasteful things such as government spending, product packaging, Adam Sandler movies, and golf. And then it hit me like a pitching wedge across the frontal lobe. Golf was the solution to the animal waste problem.
Reporter:	How so?
Roger:	Well, the goal is to get rid of animal waste, to get it off the grass and in the woods, where people won't step on it. Well, isn't that what golfers do? They eventually hit all their golf balls into the woods. Bingo! And, that was how I came to invent the animal waste golf ball, win the coveted Bronze Scooper, and earn the moniker "The Wizard of Waste."
Reporter:	Was it all that simple?
Roger:	Not exactly. There was a lot of regulating that went on—the R in SOAR—as I honed and molded the perfect golf ball . . . and a lot of hand washing.

You've learned how SOAR helps you study by **S**electing important ideas and recording complete notes, **O**rganizing notes, **A**ssociating the noted ideas to one another and to your past knowledge, and **R**egulating learning through self-testing. This chapter demonstrates how SOAR (or parts of it) helps you in three other important situations: reading, writing, and solving real-world problems.

USING SOAR FOR READING

You saw in Chapter 2 how to select important text ideas for further study. Let's now see how you might use the entire SOAR process to learn the information in the following boxed passage:

Young Marriage

The marriages with the poorest track records for success are those in which each partner is below the age of 18. Also, when both partners are school dropouts, there is little chance of success. When the female is pregnant prior to marriage, the prognosis for the marriage is also grim.

Marriages with an intermediate chance of success are characterized by females being age 17 or older and males being age 20 or older. The female

---

(*continued*)

has dropped out of high school but the male has graduated from high school. The couple does not begin marriage with a pregnancy but conceives a child immediately after the marriage.

Marriages with the best chance of success are those in which the partners are high school graduates. Pregnancy does not occur until at least one year after the marriage. The partners are older. The female is at least 18 and the male is at least 20.

As you read the passage, you should first *select* and note all the important ideas. Here is an example of how this might be done:

YOUNG MARRIAGE

Poor Track Record
> Each partner is below 18
> Both are high school dropouts
> Female pregnant before marriage

Intermediate Chance of Success
> Female age 17+
> Male age 20+
> Female dropped out of high school
> Male graduated high school
> Pregnancy occurs after marriage

Best Chance of Success
> Partners high school graduates
> Pregnancy occurs at least 1 year after marriage
> Partners older: Female 18+, male 20+

You should then *organize* the selected ideas if possible. Exhibit 8.1 shows how the noted ideas might be organized into a matrix.

Next you should create internal and external associations. Some possible ones are as follows:

Internal Associations

- The probability for a successful marriage increases as age increases, education increases, and pregnancy is delayed.

- The least successful young marriages involve partners who are below age 18, are high school dropouts, and become pregnant prior to marriage.

- The most successful young marriages involve partners who are 18 or older, are high school graduates, and conceive at least one year after marriage.

External Associations

- Becoming pregnant before marriage perhaps "forces" marriage.

- Older and more educated partners are more mature and have more earning power and thus more successful marriages.

EXHIBIT 8.1   Organized notes for passage entitled "Young Marriage."

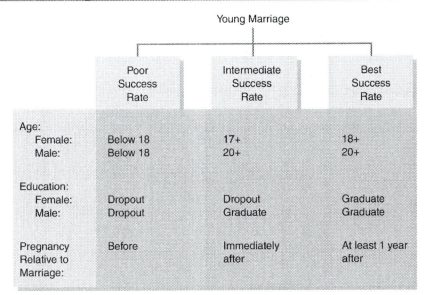

	Poor Success Rate	Intermediate Success Rate	Best Success Rate
Age:			
Female:	Below 18	17+	18+
Male:	Below 18	20+	20+
Education:			
Female:	Dropout	Dropout	Graduate
Male:	Dropout	Graduate	Graduate
Pregnancy Relative to Marriage:	Before	Immediately after	At least 1 year after

- With delayed pregnancy, there is more time to solidify the marriage and to prepare the household for a child.
- Cousin Jethro fits with poor success rate characteristics and his marriage failed.
- I wonder how children from these different marriages fare? I suppose there is a positive correlation between marriage success rate and child success.

Finally, you should regulate learning by generating and answering practice test questions. Here are some sample questions:

Test Questions

- What are the characteristics of failing marriages?
- What role does education play in marriage failure and success?
- What seems to be the key age for males in nonfailing marriages?
- What is the difference between marriages with intermediate success and best success?
- Mark and Peggy are 17-year-old high school dropouts. Peggy became pregnant and the couple subsequently married. What is the likely success rate for their marriage?

See, that's not too tough. This step-by-step example has shown you that you can SOAR to success just as well when learning from text as from lecture.

When reading, however, the SOAR components don't have to be used in a step-by-step way. Any component can easily be applied anytime it is needed. Why? What makes text learning different from lecture learning?

Lectures are fleeting; texts are permanent. Lectures are like sprints; texts are like strolls. Because lectures fly by so quickly, students have their hands full just selecting key ideas and recording them in notes. There's little time to make representations, create associations, and generate questions. Doing those things must wait for later. Not so with text. Texts just sit there like faithful dogs. While reading, you have plenty of time and opportunity to select ideas, organize them, create associations, and raise questions. Moreover, you can do these things at any time rather than one step at a time. Let me show you what I mean.

Exhibit 8.2 is a short passage about rhinos. While reading this passage, I'll use the five SOAR strategies as needed (having divided association into internal and external associations).

- Selection (S)
- Organization (O)
- Internal Association (IA)
- External Association (EA)
- Regulation (Questioning) (R)

I'll use the organization, internal association, external association, and regulation strategies as I usually would. You'll see these strategies at work in the right margin of the text. Things will be a little different for the selection strategy. Because the text is permanent, I won't select ideas by recording them in notes (although, of course, I could). There's no need to. Instead, I'll mark the text. I'll use a marking strategy to select ideas by drawing boxes around major topics, circling key categories, and underlining important facts. Of course, these are the three main parts of representations: the topics are the top portion of a hierarchy, sequence, or matrix; the categories are the words down the left side of a matrix; and the facts are the ideas within the matrix cells.

"Hold the phone," you're saying. "You told us clear back in Chapter 2 not to highlight the text. You said it was often mindlessly done and ineffective. You told us to write notes instead. Was that not true? Liar, liar, pants on fire.

Okay, settle down. I did say that highlighting is often ineffective. Students tend to highlight too much and without much thought. What I'm advocating now is not highlighting but a marking system that encourages you to select key ideas that fit within topics and categories you must also select. Moreover, by simultaneously using the other SOAR components—organization, association, and regulation—you're forced to think about the text ideas in meaningful ways. So, put down the phone and see how you might use all the SOAR strategies while reading by studying Exhibit 8.2.

EXHIBIT 8.2   *The SOAR strategies at work.*

Rhinos

The two most prevalent rhinos are the black and white rhinos.[1] Just like their contrasting colors, they are as different as night and day.

 (Location)

First, consider the black rhino of southern Africa. It weighs between 2,000 and 4,000 pounds[2] and is medium size for a rhino. It has two horns. The longer one in front can measure 52 inches.[3] The shorter horn is right behind it.

(Social)
(Habitat)

Black rhinos are solitary. They like to stay in the jungle rather than out in the open African plains.[4] It's just as well that black rhinos are loners because they are known for having bad tempers.[5] They charge more often than any other rhino species.[6]

So how do you keep a black rhino happy? Leave it alone with plenty to eat. Its favorite foods are juicy twigs and fresh young shoots from trees and bushes.[7] Black rhinos are picky eaters, which is why their hooked lips come in handy.[8] They use their hooked top lip to feel around for food and grab it. Then they chomp down with their teeth.

Organization

Rhinos

1. (O)   Black | White

2. (EA)   Weight of car
3. (EA)   Horn may be used for fighting
3. (EA)   Horn over 4 feet

3. (O)   **Rhinos**   Black | White

Location:
Horns:
4. (IA)   Easy to be solitary among the trees
5. (IA)   No one wants to be with someone with a bad temper.
6. (EA)   People with bad tempers get "charged" with crimes.

6. (O)   **Rhinos**   Black | White

Location:
Horns:
Social:
Habitat:
Temperament:
7. (EA)   Vegetarians
8. (IA)   Hooked lips grasp twigs and shoots.

8. (O)   **Rhinos**   Black | White

Location:
Horns:
Social:
Habitat:
Temperament:
Food:
Lips:

Regulation (Questioning)

Where do black rhinos live?

How much do they weigh?

How many horns do they have?

How long are their horns?

Do black rhinos live in groups?

What is their habitat?

Are black rhinos docile or aggressive?

What do black rhinos eat?

What kind of lips do black rhinos have and how do their lips help them eat?

Are white rhinos aggressive?

How much do they weigh?

Do they live alone?

Where do white rhinos live?

What is their habitat?

What do they eat?

What kind of lips do they have and how do their lips help them eat?

(continued)

177

EXHIBIT 8.2 (continued)

White rhinos, on the other hand, are more

Temperament

easygoing than black rhinos.[9] And it's a good

thing, too, since white rhinos are almost twice

as big.[10] They (weigh) between 5,000 and 8,000

pounds.[11] These animals are friendly with each

Social

other. They live in small family groups of three

to five.[12] The bulls will occasionally charge to

defend their home-range territory,[13] but white

Temperament

rhinos rarely fight.

White rhinos live primarily in northern Africa.[14]

Location

They like open grassy areas, as long as there are

Habitat

bushes for shade. They are not picky about food.

White rhinos have square (lips) which they use to

Food

graze on dry grass.[15] Like black rhinos, they have

two (horns,)[16] one in front of the other.

9. (IA)	White rhinos more easygoing
10. (IA)	Nearly twice as big as black rhinos
11. (EA)	Size of truck
12. (IA)	Live in groups; black rhino solitary
12. (EA)	3–5 in group is ideal size for study group
13. (EA)	Like most people, will only fight when provoked
14. (IA)	Northern Africa for white and southern Africa for black
14. (EA)	There are a lot of grasslands in northern Africa.
15. (IA)	Square lips help them scoop grass.
15. (EA)	White rhinos are like cows, which have square lips and eat grass.
16. (IA)	Both rhinos have two horns.
16. (O)	Both rhinos eat what is available in habitat and have lips suited for eating.

How many horns do white rhinos have?

How are black and white rhinos alike?

How are they different?

What's the relationship among habitat, lips, and food?

Rhinos

	Black	White
Location:	S. Africa	N. Africa
Horns:	2	2
Social:	Solitary	Groups
Habitat:	Jungle	Grasslands
Temperament:	Aggressive	Easygoing
Food:	Twigs & shoots	Grass
Lips:	Hooked	Square

Exercise 1

Using the text passage below, demonstrate the SOAR strategies (including text marking for selection) for learning this material.

Personality Theories

There are two major personality theories: behaviorism and humanism. I discuss each of these in turn.

Behaviorism was developed during the early 1900s in the United States. The founder of behaviorism was J. B. Watson. The central idea of behaviorism is that a person behaves in certain ways, either to receive a reward or to avoid a punishment. For example, a student will work hard on an assignment either to receive a high grade or to avoid a poor one. Behavioral therapists try to shape people's behavior by getting them to work for a reward or to avoid a punishment.

The main idea of humanism is that people behave in healthy ways when they are treated by others with dignity and respect. For example, someone who is a member of a supportive family is usually well adjusted. Therefore, therapy focuses on helping people to feel good about themselves and to treat themselves with dignity and respect. Humanism was founded by Carl Rogers in the United States during the mid-1900s.

USING SOAR FOR WRITING

When you think about it, most writing is a response to some question. Perhaps the question is an essay question posed on a test, such as "Describe the Piagetian stages of development with respect to age of onset, social characteristics, and cognitive characteristics?" Perhaps the question is one you pose when asked to write a term paper. If your assigned or chosen topic is drug abuse in sports, you might pose the question, "How has steroid use impacted major league baseball?" In this section, I'm answering the question, "How does SOAR relate to and enhance writing?"

We see, then, that writing begins with a question. This is akin to the last stage of the SOAR study system—regulation—when you anticipate and generate potential questions. Unlike studying, though, there is no doubt about what question you need to answer when writing. The writing question is clearly posed by the instructor or by you. You've seen how question generation (regulation) is part of

Writers should use SOAR to write complete, well-organized, and cohesive essays.

EXHIBIT 8.3   *Prepare the content when writing.*

	Types of Creativity		
	Adaptive	**Innovative**	**Emergent**
Outcome:	Solving a common problem in a new way	Creating a new or improved product	Reshaping the direction of a discipline
Motivation:	External	External	Internal
Time Demands:	3–5 years	5–10 years	10 or more years

studying and writing. Now, let's see how the other SOAR components are used in writing.

Let's suppose you are taking a psychology test and are given the following essay item: "Compare the three types of creativity with respect to outcome, motivation, and time demands."

To generate a complete and well-organized response, you must first select and organize the content (the *S* and *O* in SOAR). You can do so by creating a complete matrix representation like that in Exhibit 8.3. That representation provides all of the necessary information in an organized form to prepare you for writing your response.

Of course, it's just as easy to misuse that representation in Exhibit 8.3 as it is to use it properly when writing an essay answer. Let me show you two common misuses. One misuse is to describe each type of creativity in turn. For example, "Adaptive creativity involves solving a common problem in a new way; it involves internal motivation; and it takes three to five years to develop. Innovative creativity . . . " This topic-by-topic approach fails to compare and contrast the topics as directed. A second misuse involves "writing across the topics" but in a piece-by-piece fashion—and failing to connect the pieces. For example, "The time demand for adaptive creativity is 3–5 years. The time demand for innovative creativity is 5–10 years. The time demand for emergent creativity is 10 or more years."

Properly using the representation depends on creating associations (the *A* in SOAR) among facts in order to articulate the comparisons and contrasts. Reexamine Exhibit 8.3 and you'll note these important internal associations:

- The creative outcomes appear progressively more sophisticated going from adaptive (solving a common problem) to innovative (creating or improving a product) to emergent (reshaping a discipline).

- External motivation is associated with the two least sophisticated types of creativity (adaptive and innovative), whereas internal motivation is associated with the most sophisticated type of creativity (emergent).

- External motivation is associated with types of creativity (adaptive and innovative) that arise from the environment (an external source), whereas internal motivation is associated with emergent creativity that arises from one's own ideas and thoughts (an internal source).

- As the types of creativity increase in sophistication, the time demands for becoming creative increase linearly as well.

These internal associations become the foundation of your written response to the test item asking you to compare and contrast the three types of creativity with respect to outcome, motivation, and time demands.

How do external connections play a role in answering the creativity item? In one way, they don't. The internal associations are sufficient for forming an answer to this compare-and-contrast item. But, in another way, external associations do play a role. Including external associations such as the following illustrates your command of the subject and makes for a more interesting and informative answer:

- Coming up with a new system for doing laundry is an example of adaptive creativity.

- Creating a new defensive system in soccer is an example of innovative creativity.

- Sigmund Freud's discovery of psychoanalysis reshaped the discipline of psychology and is an example of emergent creativity.

Pulling the SOAR components together, you might respond to the creativity item as follows:

> The three types of creativity—adaptive, innovative, and emergent—differ with respect to outcomes, motivation, and time demands. I compare and contrast the three types along each dimension in turn. I conclude with general observations about how the types are similar and different.
>
> The three types of creativity differ with respect to the outcomes produced. The three types—going from adaptive to innovative to emergent—increase in sophistication. Adaptive creativity involves solving a common problem in a new way such as coming up with a better system for doing laundry. Innovative creativity is more sophisticated. It involves inventing or improving a product. An example might be developing a better defensive system in soccer. Emergent creativity is the most sophisticated. It involves reshaping an entire discipline. When Sigmund Freud invented psychoanalysis, this development changed the course of psychology.

In line with this progression of outcomes is the progression of years necessary to achieve the outcomes. As the type of creativity grows in sophistication, so, too, does the number of years necessary to become creative: adaptive, 3–5 years; innovative, 5–10 years; and emergent, 10 or more years. Thus, the more sophisticated the outcome, the longer the time demand to become creative.

The motivation for the types of creativity stems from either internal or external sources. The source of motivation is external for adaptive and innovative creativity, but internal for emergent. The source of motivation seems consistent with the outcome. Adaptively creative people and innovatively creative people are concerned with solving problems that arise from the environment (e.g., the need to do laundry more efficiently or play better defense)—an external source. Emergently creative people, by contrast, are concerned with their own thoughts and ideas about a discipline (e.g., how psychoanalysis can improve psychology)—an internal source.

In conclusion, it is evident that the three types of creativity differ with respect to the sophistication of the creative product. These differences correspond to the time demands for creating the creative product. The more sophisticated the product, the longer it takes to create it. Most creative products, meanwhile, stem from external sources such as everyday problems or the need to build a better mousetrap. Only the most sophisticated type of creativity (emergent) depends on an internal motivation to reshape the direction of an entire discipline.

One more thing about writing and SOAR. A question like the creativity one should never be a surprise on test day. An effective SOAR studier would of course regulate learning; he or she would anticipate this question and prepare a complete, organized, and integrated essay well in advance of the test.

Exercise 2

Use the SOAR components to generate and answer an essay question about the DIFS motivational model discussed in Chapter 7.

USING SOAR FOR SOLVING REAL-WORLD PROBLEMS

You might think that learning and studying end when you graduate from college, law school, medical school, or trade school, but that's when it really just begins. You must continue learning at your job to stay with the times or ahead of them. Attorneys build case knowledge by poring over law books. Medical doctors stay current on medical procedures and drug treatments by carefully reading medical journals and attending seminars. Auto mechanics study repair manuals that detail the parts and processes of a new braking system or an antiquated transmission.

Outside work, learning continues. Pursuing a hobby such as chess or photography requires a lot of study. Consider that more books have been written about chess than all other games combined. Should you choose to remodel your kitchen or bathroom, you must learn about construction, plumbing, city codes, and building permits.

Sometimes learning is not by choice but by necessity. Perhaps a relative develops multiple sclerosis, bears a child with Down syndrome, or is stricken with Alzheimer's disease. Now you must study these afflictions and learn how to cope with them. The better you learn, the better you work, play, and live.

Here's an example of how I once used the organization component of SOAR in a real-world setting. I used to have a Honda Accord. I called it my Honda Discord. It was rust—no not rust colored, just rust. It was not the most dependable of cars either. It was about as dependable as single-ply tissue. Anyway, I took it in for service to a place a friend recommended that charges only for parts and labor. Tell me I don't know a deal when I see one. I ended up getting an oil change and work done on the sound system, cooling system, horn, clutch, and fuel filters. The glove compartment was broken too, but I decided to let that go because I rarely wore gloves.

SOAR can help you learn more about your job.

When the repairs were completed, a worker handed me the two-page bill shown in Exhibit 8.4. I had problems with this bill beyond those associated with cost—$21.60 to drain and fill the radiator. Ridiculous. Next time, I'll get our five-year-old neighbor boy to do it. The main problem I had with the bill, though, was that it separated parts and labor costs. I couldn't easily tell what a particular job, such as flushing the cooling system, was actually costing me. So, I reorganized the information into the single matrix representation shown in Exhibit 8.5. Now I could quickly and easily see what each job cost in terms of both parts and labor.

Attaining this personal insight was not enough for this educational psychologist. I felt the urge—perhaps the calling—to teach others. So I called together all the workers. "Quick, everybody come look at this," I bellowed over the roar of tuned engines and the rumble of lug-nut wrenches. Once cars were lowered from their jacks and workers all assembled, I proudly flashed the matrix and began extolling its virtues. I think they really liked the idea and wanted it to spread. They told me I should take my car somewhere else next time.

Let's move next to another more serious illustration showing how someone just five years out of college used SOAR strategies to plot an investment plan that will eventually make him a millionaire. Listen in as David tells his story. (The italicized statements in parentheses show how portions of SOAR were used.)

EXHIBIT 8.4   *Poorly organized car repair bill.*

Car Repair

Page 1 (Labor)

Replace fuel filters	$ 7.20
Flush cooling system	21.60
Adjust clutch	7.20
Repair horn	14.40
Replace antenna	18.00
Replace speakers	21.60

Page 2 (Parts)

Antennae	$14.99
Oil filter	5.20
Oil	4.80
Fuel filter (a)	4.38
Fuel filter (b)	7.76
Antifreeze	11.00
Speakers	79.10

EXHIBIT 8.5   *Well-organized car repair bill.*

Car Repair

	Labor	Parts	Total
Fuel filters	$ 7.20	$ 12.14	$ 19.34
Cooling system	21.60	11.00	32.60
Clutch	7.20		7.20
Horn	14.40		14.40
Antennae	18.00	14.99	32.99
Speakers	21.60	79.10	100.70
Oil change		10.00	10.00
TOTAL	$90.00	$127.23	$217.23

I'm David, a 26-year-old nurse making about $40,000 a year. I own a small home and drive an old but dependable car. I have about $10,000 in savings, which is available for emergencies. For the present, I'm neither rich nor poor—I'm comfortable. My financial future, however, is bright. When I retire in 30 or 40 years, I will be a millionaire. I am not planning on winning the

EXHIBIT 8.6   *Representation showing the value of early investing.*

	Anna	Sam
Age at Initial Investment:	21	40
Investment Plan:	$2,000 each year for 5 years	$2,000 each year for 25 years
Total Invested:	$10,000	$50,000
Retirement Savings (Age 65):	$608,000	$230,000

lottery or receiving a huge inheritance. I'm not a broker or a soothsayer. I have no financial training and no crystal ball. I have simply made a few smart financial decisions, guided by SOAR strategies.

When I was 21 and about to graduate from nursing school, I saw a representation in a magazine that convinced me to open a retirement account immediately. The chart, shown in Exhibit 8.6, illustrates the value of early savings. The chart shows that Anna invested $2,000 for 5 consecutive years, resulting in a $10,000 investment. Sam invested $2,000 for 25 consecutive years, resulting in a $50,000 investment. Anna wisely began investing when she was only 21. Sam began investing when he was 40. Each retired a. age 65. Sam's $50,000 investment had grown to $230,000. Not bad. Anna's meager $10,000 investment now equaled a whopping $608,000. (Both investments earned an average yield of 10 percent per year.) I did the math and I figured that if I invested just $2,000 each year beginning at age 21, at retirement I would accumulate about $1.5 million from my $88,000 investment. (*Have you noticed some SOAR components so far? The chart in Exhibit 8.6 is good organization. David's analysis of the chart involved internal associations, and David's application of investment ideas to his own life involved external associations.*)

Having decided to save for retirement, I next decided *how* to save. My parents had money socked away in savings accounts and certificates of deposit (CDs) and recommended I do the same. Before heeding their advice, I browsed through a few financial magazines and learned that there are three primary investment sources: savings accounts and CDs, stocks, and bonds. After reading about these investment sources, I developed the representation shown in Exhibit 8.7. Doing so helped me plot my investment strategy. (*David selected and organized information.*)

I learned from Exhibit 8.7 that savings accounts and CDs, despite my parents' endorsement, are a dead-end road for long-term growth. My parents should be enjoying their golden years, but because of overly conservative investments, they are just scraping by. (*David makes an external association.*) I chose stocks because they offered the greatest opportunity for growth. Although they are riskier than bonds in the short run, they outperform bonds in the long run. (*David makes internal associations.*)

EXHIBIT 8.7   *Representation for choosing type of investment.*

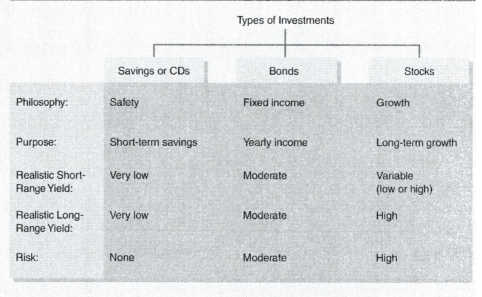

Types of Investments

	Savings or CDs	Bonds	Stocks
Philosophy:	Safety	Fixed income	Growth
Purpose:	Short-term savings	Yearly income	Long-term growth
Realistic Short-Range Yield:	Very low	Moderate	Variable (low or high)
Realistic Long-Range Yield:	Very low	Moderate	High
Risk:	None	Moderate	High

EXHIBIT 8.8   *Representation showing stock investment options.*

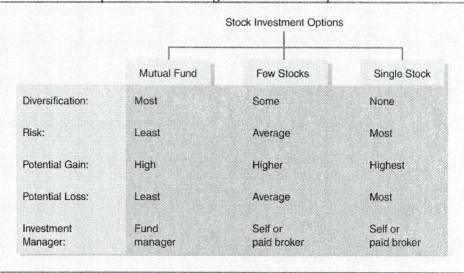

Stock Investment Options

	Mutual Fund	Few Stocks	Single Stock
Diversification:	Most	Some	None
Risk:	Least	Average	Most
Potential Gain:	High	Higher	Highest
Potential Loss:	Least	Average	Most
Investment Manager:	Fund manager	Self or paid broker	Self or paid broker

After deciding to invest in stocks, I next considered whether to invest in a single stock, a few stocks, or a mutual fund that invests in several stocks. Again, I looked up information about these options, and developed the stock investments representation shown in Exhibit 8.8 (*selection and organization*).

EXHIBIT 8.9   Representation displaying types of mutual funds.

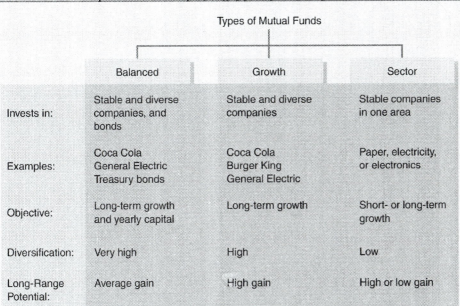

	Balanced	Growth	Sector
Invests in:	Stable and diverse companies, and bonds	Stable and diverse companies	Stable companies in one area
Examples:	Coca Cola General Electric Treasury bonds	Coca Cola Burger King General Electric	Paper, electricity, or electronics
Objective:	Long-term growth and yearly capital	Long-term growth	Short- or long-term growth
Diversification:	Very high	High	Low
Long-Range Potential:	Average gain	High gain	High or low gain

After I'd examined Exhibit 8.8, I chose to invest in mutual funds. I didn't want to manage my stock investments because I had neither the time nor the expertise (*external association*). Nor did I want to pay a broker. Having a professional manager invest my money was appealing.

Other factors that favored mutual funds apparent in Exhibit 8.8 were diversification and reduced risk. A mutual fund that invests in several stocks poses less risk than investing directly in a single stock or a few stocks. Although a mutual fund has less potential for growth than a single stock, it still offers wonderful growth potential with fewer risks (*internal associations*).

My next decision determined my choice of the type of mutual fund that I thought was best for me. I learned that there are three major types: balanced, growth, and sector. I developed Exhibit 8.9 to compare them (*selects and organizes ideas*).

After analyzing the types of mutual funds, I chose to invest in growth funds. Sector funds lacked diversification and appeared too risky compared with the others (*internal association*). They could either hit a home run or strike out (*external association*). Furthermore, a smart investor invests in sector funds before they're "hot" and while prices are low. I had little faith that I could predict advancing sectors (*external association*). Furthermore, the sector market is volatile and needs to be watched closely. I preferred a more

EXHIBIT 8.10　Representation displaying top-performing growth funds.

Top-Performing Growth Funds				
A	B	C	D	E
Average Total Return:				
Last Year: 19.37	32.61	17.38	24.83	22.77
5 Years: —	—	16.34	20.64	18.34
10 Years: —	—	19.44	14.23	17.92
Risk: Average	Above average	Average	Above average	Average
Performance in Bull Market: *****	*****	***	*****	****
Performance in Bear Market: ?	?	***	**	***
Minimum Investment: $1,000	$2,500	$250	$1,000	$250
Load: 3%	3%	None	None	None
Manager Stability: 1 year	1 year	2 years	6 years	10 years

stable investment (*external association*). The balanced funds were appealing, but because I was young and could ride out fluctuations in growth funds, I chose growth funds because of their historically higher long-term gains (*internal and external associations*).

The last decision was selecting a specific growth fund. I located a publication that listed the performance of all mutual funds. From that listing I constructed Exhibit 8.10, which compares last year's top-performing growth funds (*selection and organization*).

Using Exhibit 8.10, I chose Fund E. I preferred it for several reasons. First, its risk was average. I felt uncomfortable selecting the overly risky funds B and D (*external associations*). Second, the fund's minimum investment of $250 was appealing. This meant that I could make eight monthly investments of $250 to reach my $2,000 investment objective (*external associations*). Third, I liked Fund E's no-load system. No-load funds have no investment fee. The 3 percent loads charged by Funds A and B would actually reduce my yearly $2,000 investment to $1,940 (*external associations*).

Perhaps most appealing was Fund E's relative stability (*internal association*). It had been managed by the same person for 10 years. I read that the manager was 34 years old and planned to continue managing the fund for some time. Another indicator of stability was the fund's solid performance over the past 10 years. Other funds (such as A and B) had much shorter track records or were less profitable (Fund D) (*internal associations*). Fund E's stability over 10 years reflected its solid performance in both bull (upward) and bear (downward) markets (*internal associations*). The previous seven years were predominantly bull markets, but the three years before that were bear markets (*external associations*). Strong 10-year growth reflected Fund E's performance in both bull and bear markets (*internal associations*). Also, its four- and three-star ratings (out of a possible five-star rating) for bull and bear markets, respectively, confirmed its stability in varied market conditions (*internal associations*).

Since I drew up this plan and began investing, I've made some necessary changes. Unlike school, there is no paper-and-pencil test to prepare for in the real world. But, just as students must anticipate and prepare for tests, as an investor I've had to anticipate and prepare for changing conditions that call for changes in my investment plan (*regulates learning*). For instance, when I saw the economy head south, I moved some of my holdings into conservative funds. When I got married and had more income, my wife began investing more than $2,000 yearly. We like the ring of "millionaires."

Exercise 3

Try using SOAR strategies to solve this real-world problem.

You are looking for an apartment. You've visited several and taken a few notes. Which one will you choose?

APARTMENT NOTES

Cromwell Drive	Rainbow Circle	Zoo Street
Half mile to school	Fireplace	1 bedroom
$525/month	Health club	650 square feet
460 square feet	4 miles to work	Deck
Wooded area	1.5 miles to school	6 miles to work
2 miles to work	$550/month	3 miles to school
Covered parking	1 bedroom	Busy street
1 bedroom	Nice neighborhood	Fresh paint
	Noisy neighbors	$625/month
	580 square feet	Fireplace

SUMMARY

This chapter illustrated how SOAR strategies can be used for more than learning lecture content. They are instrumental for reading, writing, and solving real-world problems.

When reading, readers should select important text information by marking it in the text. Concurrently, they should organize the key ideas by creating representations. Readers should also note internal and external associations while reading. Moreover, readers should regulate learning by generating and answering potential test questions.

When writing, writers should write in response to some question. Question recognition or generation is akin to the regulation phase (R) of SOAR. Writers should select (S) and organize (O) ideas needed for writing. They should write cohesively by joining and communicating related ideas (internal associations [A]) and perhaps elaborate by providing examples and evaluative comments (external associations [A]).

Solving real-world problems is a reality. You must solve work and personal problems frequently. SOAR can help because problem solving involves selecting and organizing relevant information, uncovering patterns or associations in that information, associating it with your own situation, and testing your plan in the real world.

ANSWERS TO FOCUS QUESTIONS

1. Lectures are fleeting. When learning from lectures, students barely have time to select ideas and record complete notes. Applying the other SOAR components must usually wait until after the lecture. Not so with texts, which are permanent. Students can take their time and apply all the SOAR components—at any time—while they read.

2. Students can select important text information by marking key ideas. Specifically, they can put boxes around topics, circle categories, and underline facts.

3. Almost all writing begins with a question. The writer strives to answer a question imposed by others or by oneself.

4. Writing is done in response to a question. Question generation and response is akin to regulating learning (R). Writers must have all the relevant information needed to answer the question in an organized form. This is akin to selecting and organizing information (S and O). Writers must also communicate relationships among ideas (internal associations [A]) and often add examples or associate ideas with outside things (external associations [A]) to make writing more understandable and interesting.

5. SOAR can help employees learn more about doing their jobs, no matter what the job is. SOAR can help people pursue hobbies such as photography or chess. It can help people deal with serious problems such as multiple sclerosis and mundane problems such as remodeling a kitchen.

6. You can use SOAR to learn about and apply financial information. You can do this by selecting important information and organizing it in several representations, making internal associations among ideas and external associations with previous knowledge to reach sound financial decisions, and regulating real-world investments by monitoring their success and making changes in your investment plan accordingly.

Supplemental Readings

Atkinson, R. K., Levin, J. R., Kiewra, K. A., Meyers, T., Kim, S., Atkinson, L., Renandya, W. A., & Hwang, Y. (1999). Matrix and mnemonic text-processing adjuncts: Comparing and combining their components. *Journal of Educational Psychology, 91,* 342–357.

Barnett, J. E., DiVesta, F. J., & Rogozinski, J. T. (1981). What is learned in note taking? *Journal of Educational Psychology, 73,* 181–192.

Benton, S. L., Kiewra, K. A., Whitfall, J., & Dennison, R. (1993). Encoding and external-storage effects on writing processes. *Journal of Educational Psychology, 85,* 267–280.

Blanchard, J. S. (1985). What to tell students about underlining … and why. *Journal of Reading, 29,* 199–203.

Bransford, J. D., Brown, A. L., & Cocking, R. (Eds.). (1999). *How people learn.* Washington, DC: National Academy Press.

Brown, A. L., & Day, J. D. (1983). Macrorules for summarizing texts: The development of expertise. *Journal of Verbal Learning and Verbal Behavior, 22,* 1–14.

Brown, A. L., Campione, J. C., & Barclay, C. R. (1979). Training self-checking routines for estimating test readiness: Generalization from list learning to prose recall. *Child Development, 50,* 501–512.

Brown, L. (1992). *Live your dreams.* New York: HarperCollins.

Chi, M. T. H., & Bassok, M. (1989). Learning from examples via self-explanations. In L. B. Resnick (Ed.), *Knowing, learning, and instruction* (pp. 251–282). Hillsdale, NJ: Lawrence Erlbaum.

Chi, M. T. H., De Leeuw, N., Chiu, M. H., & La Vancher, C. (1994). Eliciting self-explanations improves understanding. *Cognitive Science, 18,* 439–477.

Cognition and Technology Group at Vanderbilt. (1992). The Jasper series as an example of anchored instruction: Theory, program description, and assessment data. *Educational Psychologist, 27,* 291–315.

Craik, F., & Watkins, M. (1973). The role of rehearsal in short-term memory. *Journal of Verbal Learning and Verbal Behavior, 12,* 599–607.

Csikszentmihalyi, M. (1996). *Creativity: Flow and the psychology of discovery and invention.* New York: HarperCollins.

Derry, S. J. (1984). Effects of an organizer on memory for prose. *Journal of Educational Psychology, 76,* 98–107.

Ericsson, K. A. (1996). *The road to excellence: The acquisition of expert performance in the arts and sciences, sports and games.* Mahwah, NJ: Lawrence Erlbaum.

Gagne, R. M. (1968). Learning hierarchies. *Educational Psychologist, 6,* 1–9.

Gagne, R. M. (1985). *The conditions of learning* (4th ed.). New York: Holt, Rinehart, and Winston.

Gall, M. D., Gall, J. P., Jacobson, D. R., & Bullock, T. L. (1990). *Tools for learning: A guide to teaching study skills.* Alexandria, VA: Association for Supervision and Curriculum Development.

Gardner, H. (1997). *Extraordinary minds: Portraits of 4 exceptional individuals and an examination of our own extraordinariness.* New York: Basic Books.

Graham, S. (1991). A review of attribution theory in achievement contexts. *Educational Psychology Review, 3,* 5–39.

Gubbels, P. S. (1999). *College student studying: A collective case study.* Unpublished doctoral dissertation, University of Nebraska–Lincoln.

Hayes, J. R., & Flower, L. S. (1986). Writing research and the writer. *American Psychologist, 41,* 1106–1113.

Johnson, D. W., & Johnson, R. T. (1985). The internal dynamics of cooperative learning groups. In R. Slavin, S. Sharan, S. Kagan, C. Webb, & R. Schmuck (Eds.), *Learning to cooperate, cooperating to learn* (pp. 103–124). New York: Plenum.

Jonassen, D. H., Beissner, K., & Yacci, M. (1993). *Structural knowledge: Techniques for representing, conveying, and acquiring structural knowledge.* Hillsdale, NJ: Erlbaum.

Kiewra, K. A. (1987). Notetaking and review: The research and its implications. *Journal of Instructional Science, 16,* 233–249.

Kiewra, K. A. (1989). A review of note taking. The encoding-storage paradigm and beyond. *Educational Psychology Review, 1,* 147–172.

Kiewra, K. A. (1991). Aids to lecture learning. *Educational Psychologist, 26,* 37–54.

Kiewra, K. A. (1994). The matrix representation system: Orientation, research, theory and application. In J. Smart (Ed.), *Higher education: Handbook of theory and research* (pp. 331–373). New York: Agathon.

Kiewra, K. A., & Creswell, J. W. (2000). Conversations with three highly productive educational psychologists: Richard Anderson, Richard Mayer, and Michael Pressley. *Educational Psychology Review, 12,* 135–161.

Kiewra, K. A., DuBois, N. F., Christian, D., & McShane, A. (1988). Providing study notes: A comparison of three types of notes for review. *Journal of Educational Psychology, 80,* 595–597.

Kiewra, K. A., DuBois, N. F., Christian, D., McShane, A., Meyerhoffer, M., & Roskelley, D. (1991). Notetaking functions and techniques. *Journal of Educational Psychology, 83,* 240–245.

Kiewra, K. A., Kauffman, D. F., Robinson, D., DuBois, N., & Staley, R. K. (1999). Supplementing floundering text with adjunct displays. *Journal of Instructional Science, 27,* 373–401.

Kiewra, K. A., Mayer, R. E., Christensen, M., Kim, S., & Risch, N. (1991). Effects of repetition on recall and notetaking: Strategies for learning from lectures. *Journal of Educational Psychology, 83,* 120–123.

Kiewra, K. A., O'Connor, T., McCrudden, M., & Liu, X. (2001). *Developing young chess masters: What are the right moves?* Paper presented at the Koltanowski Memorial Conference on Chess in Education, Dallas, TX.

Killigrew, B. (May, 1999). Player of the month: Maurice Ashley. *Chess Life, 54*(5): 340–342.

King, A. (1992). Comparison of self questioning, summarizing, and notetaking-review as strategies for learning from lectures. *American Educational Research Journal, 29,* 303–323.

Larkin, J. H., & Simon, H. A. (1987). Why a diagram is (sometimes) worth 10,000 words. *Cognitive Science, 11*(1), 65–100.

Levin, J. R. (1981). The mnemonic '80s: Keywords in the classroom. *Educational Psychologist, 16,* 65–82.

Levin, J. R., & Mayer, R. E. (1993). Understanding illustrations in text. In B. K. Britton, A. Woodward, & M. Binkley (Eds.), *Learning from textbooks: Theory and practice* (pp. 95–113). Hillsdale, NJ: Erlbaum.

Lorch, R. F. (1989). Text-signaling devices and their effects on reading and memory processes. *Educational Psychology Review, 1,* 209–234.

Marxen, D. E. (1996). Why reading and underlining a passage is a less effective strategy than simply rereading the passage. *Reading Improvement, 33,* 88–96.

Mayer, R. E. (1980). Elaboration techniques that increase the meaningfulness of technical text: An experimental test of the learning strategy hypothesis. *Journal of Educational Psychology, 72,* 770–784.

Mayer, R. E. (1984). Aids to prose comprehension. *Educational Psychologist, 19,* 30–42.

Mayer, R. E. (1989). Models for understanding. *Review of Educational Research, 59,* 43–64.

Mayer, R. E. (1993). Illustrations that instruct. In R. Glaser (Ed.), *Advances in instructional psychology: Volume 4* (pp. 253–284). Hillsdale, NJ: Lawrence Erlbaum.

Mayer, R. E. (1996). Learning strategies for making sense out of expository text: The SOI model for guiding three cognitive processes in knowledge construction. *Educational Psychology Review, 8,* 357–371.

Mayer, R. E. (2001). *Multimedia learning.* New York: Cambridge University Press.

Mayer, R. E. (2003). *Learning and instruction.* Upper Saddle River, NJ: Merrill Prentice Hall.

Neisser, U. (1982). *Memory observed.* San Francisco: W. H. Freeman.

Ormrod, J. E. (2003). *Educational psychology: Developing learners* (4th ed.). Upper Saddle River, NJ: Pearson Education.

Palinscar, A. S. (1986). Metacognitive strategy instruction. *Exceptional Children, 53,* 118–124.

Peper, R., & Mayer, R. E. (1978). Note taking as a generative activity. *Journal of Educational Psychology, 70,* 514–522.

Peterson, L., & Peterson, M. (1959). Short-term retention of individual verbal items. *Journal of Experimental Psychology, 58,* 193–198.

Peterson, S. E. (1992). The cognitive functions of underlining as a study technique. *Reading Research and Instruction, 31,* 49–56.

Pintrich, P. R., & De Groot, E. V. (1990). Motivational and self-regulated learning components of classroom academic performance. *Journal of Educational Psychology, 82,* 33–40.

Pintrich, P. R., & Schunk, D. H. (1996). *Motivation and education: Theory, research and applications.* Englewood Cliffs, NJ: Prentice Hall.

Pressley, M., Levin, J. R., & McCormick, C. B. (1980). Young children's learning of foreign language vocabulary: A sentence variation of the keyword method. *Contemporary Educational Psychology, 5,* 22–29.

Pressley, M., Woloshyn, V., & Associates. (1995). *Cognitive strategy instruction that really improves children's academic performance* (2nd ed.). Cambridge, MA: Brookline Books.

Rickards, J. P. (1980). Note taking, underlining, inserted questions, and organizers in text: Research conclusions and educational implications. *Educational Technology, 20,* 5–11.

Robinson, D., & Kiewra, K. A. (1995). Visual argument: Graphic organizers are superior to outlines in improving learning from text. *Journal of Educational Psychology, 87,* 455–467.

Rothkopf, E. Z. (1970). The concept of mathemagenic activites. *Review of Educational Research, 40,* 325–336.

Scardamalia, M., & Bereiter, C. (1985). Fostering the development of self-regulation in children's knowldege processing. In S. F. Chipman, J. W. Segal, & R. Glaser (Eds.), *Thinking and learning skills: Research and open questions* (pp. 563–577). Hillsdale, NJ: Lawrence Erlbaum.

Slavin, R. (1990). *Cooperative learning: Theory, research, and practice.* Englewood Cliffs, NJ: Prentice Hall.

Slotte, V., & Lonka, K. (1999). Review and process effects of spontaneous note taking on text comprehension. *Contemporary Educational Psychology, 24,* 1–20.

Solomon, G., & Perkins, D. N. (1989). Rocky roads transfer: Rethinking mechanisms of a neglected phenomenon. *Educational Psychologist, 18,* 42–50.

Spiegel, G. F., & Barufaldi, J. P. (1994). The effects of a contribution of text structure awareness and graphic postorganizers on recall and retention of science knowledge. *Journal of Research in Science Teaching, 31,* 913–932.

Spires, H. A. (1993). Learning from a lecture: Effects of comprehension monitoring. *Reading Research and Instruction, 32,* 19–30.

Titsworth, S., & Kiewra, K. A. (in press). Organizational lecture cues and student notetaking. *Contemporary Educational Psychology.*

Weiner, B. (1985). An attributional theory of achievement motivation. *Psychological Review, 92,* 548–573.

Weinstein, C. E., & Mayer R. E. (1986). The teaching of learning strategies. In M. C. Wittrock (Ed.), *Handbook of research and teaching* (3rd ed.) (pp. 315–327). New York: Macmillan.

Weisberg, R. W. (1973). *Creativity: Beyond the myth of genius.* New York: W. H. Freeman.

Wittrock, M. C. (1990). Generative processes of comprehension. *Educational Psychologist, 24,* 345–376.

Wood, E., Pressley, M., & Winne, P. (1990). Elaborative interrogation effects on children's learning of factual content. *Journal of Educational Psychology, 82,* 741–748.

Index